THE best OF MISSOURI hands

JAMES BARKSDALE
Heritage Collection

Specialty: High-quality, hand-carved one-of-a-kind shorebirds made from Missouri woods.
Media used: Basswood and sugar pine.

The sounds of the ocean and shorebirds emanate from Willie Mole's Antique Shop in Steelville, the population center of the United States. Here, full-time hobbyist James Barksdale is busy freeing a bird form from a curved piece of sugar pine.

Small coastal shorebirds are the main carving interest for Jim. He researches his pieces by poring over volumes on decoys as well as bird identification books by Audubon and Roger Tory Peterson. Not only are his birds color correct, but historically correct as well.

Today his carvings serve as ornamental fixtures in homes, but they are modeled after hunting decoys that were used heavily in the 1800s up and down the East Coast, until the 1912 passing of the Migratory Bird Act.

Jim's lifelike seabird decoys authentically rekindle this bygone era. Sandpipers, avocets, yellowlegs, curlews, woodcocks and dowitchers are familiar decoys, painted in subdued hues of grey and tan. Jim also puts holes in his decoys, simulating the wear these decoys received.

"These decoys were used to draw in the birds. The hunters actually shot the birds on the ground. So, the decoys got as many shot in 'em as the birds did," Jim said.

Jim carves both full-bodied birds and "flatties," which are thinner silhouettes of the birds, and were easier for hunters to carry and store.

In his Antique Series, Jim follows age-old traditions of using readily available materials in his decoys, such as tack eyes, cut-nail bills and distressed finishes. "Some have a nail for a beak... this one's got a bent gutter nail for a snout."

A unique krackled finish also gives carvings an aged patina. The acrylic series is to give a more realistic look to his carvings.

"I can do the same bird, the same pose, but they never turn out the same." Jim carved his first piece of wood some 40 years ago, but it wasn't until 15 years ago on a trip to Branson that he picked up the idea of carving shorebirds.

"That's always the first thing people ask, 'Are you from the coast?' Well, I've lived in Missouri all my life. I just really enjoy the shorebirds. There's such a variety. Everybody's doing ducks. I'm one of the very few who work with shorebirds. My pedestals of driftwood also really make mine stand out from those of other carvers.

"Antique shorebird decoys have become very collectable, with some selling for over $100,000 at auctions."

He cites *Best of Missouri's Hands* and several trade shows as the keys to building his hobby into a career. His work was also recently featured in *Midwest Living* magazine. His work is sold at Willie Mole's in Steelville and Bluestem Missouri Crafts in Columbia.

THE best OF MISSOURI hands™

Profiles of the State's Fine Artists and Craftsmen

Written and photographed
by Brett Dufur

Pebble Publishing
Columbia, Missouri

This book is dedicated to
the artists of Missouri

whose work reflects
a passionate heart, excellence in craftsmanship
and whose ultimate joy is working with their hands.

We are proud to call them. . . .
Best of Missouri Hands.

The craftsman can help our culture rediscover what wonderful things we can do with our eyes, our hearts and, of course, our hands.

— Martin Ratermann,
Woodworker

Acknowledgments

A warm thank you to
Best of Missouri Hands
donors and sponsors!

Contents

Preface	*ii*
Introduction	*iv*
Purpose Statement	*v*
History of the Association	*v*
Making It All Happen	*vi*
Ordering Information	*vii*
Profiles of Juried Members	1
Juried Member Addresses	105
Full Membership List	115
Associate Members	122
Donors and Sponsoring Members	123
MABDA Board of Directors	124
MABDA Past Presidents	124
Annual Conference	125
Membership Information	126
Missouri Shops and Galleries	128
Index	132
Book Ordering Information	134

Preface

Producing this book has been a whirlwind tour of the world of art and craft tradition still very much alive in Missouri. Behind the profiles that lie within these covers, I've driven over 2,000 miles bouncing off the Missouri borders like a pinball in search of the next artist around the bend.

This project took me from Mexico to Cuba (on one tank of gas) and back. I did U'ies on UU, I zipped across Z, I bought sweet peaches, 'maters and a melon.

On the road, I've seen round barns and passed square people. I drove within miles of Success and Romance. I passed Flat, Enon, Vida and Blue Eye as the miles passed by, surviving on nothing but ice cream cones and relentless barbeque. I otherwise ate, slept and lived in my truck.

I've dead-ended many a gravel road looking for the "white farm house on the left." I unknowingly memorized many a country song, swerved around slow armadillos and even saw a kid on top of a street sign holding a garage sale sign. I went.

I've beheld idyllic mist-shrouded Ozark valleys, met tired old porch dogs, heard exotic birds and been warmly received by all the folks featured here. Why, even the highway patrol stopped me several times and asked for my autograph — before the book's even out!

The artists within have a lot of passion and drive to share. I've visited every type of studio imaginable, from renovated chicken coops to designer mansions in St. Louis. It was exciting to see so many individuals succeeding and making a living doing what they do best. Most have chosen distant country roads to ply their craft, creating havens for silent studio work and creativity.

Many Best of Missouri Hands members practice age-old trades. Many continue weaving and carving traditions begun hundreds of years ago. They are the latest evolutions in timeless practicums, adding their own unique twist of verve to the slow metronome of time and tradition.

The Best of Missouri Hands organization has a well-established record for bringing Missouri's finest to the light of our appreciation. Many thanks go to the artists who have taken the time to help me compile this book.

Perhaps even as important as the artists to these pages are the countless friends and family members behind each successful artistic expression. They are perhaps far from the limelight, but their unsung efforts have allowed many Best of Missouri Hands members to follow their muse, grow artistically and succeed with their business ventures.

The following profiled members have been juried into the Best of Missouri Hands organization. Profiles are limited to the nature of their art form and their lives, since to list the exhibition records and awards received by each would become a book in itself. Most have received national and international recognition for their work, many as a result of previous Best of Missouri Hands publications.

This book is about the artists and their lives, but you'll be surprised at the history lessons you'll subconsciously absorb as each craftsmen explains the history of their craft. Beware! You may find yourself dropping words like *scherenschnitte* casually into conversation.

The artists here highlight their work, but the pictures don't tell the whole story. Instead of producing a book full of bowls, like some crafts books do, we've profiled the artists behind the work.

They represent the only constant, since their work today is different from two years ago, and will continue to evolve. It makes more sense to introduce the person behind the passion.

This book is interactive! Use this book as a reference and a catalog. Tuck it in your glove box and peruse it as you head out on your next roadtrip across the state, or to help you plan your next exploration.

In the back of the book, you'll find listings of artists with shops and studios open to the public. A listing of Missouri galleries is also given in the back to aid your search for Best of Missouri Hands products. Look for their products at these galleries and, of course, feel free to contact them directly. Businesses and shop owners wishing to stock Best of Missouri Hands products or give them as gifts are also encouraged to contact each artist.

I hope you'll help pass the word about these artists, who continue to ply age-old traditions and media with determination and artistic flare. Show your support for them by purchasing one of their works of art or by visiting their gallery. They keep alive a valuable part of our heritage, allowing us to touch a bit of the past and share it with a bit of the future.

Brett Dufur
Pebble Publishing
Rocheport, MO

Introduction

The art and craft movement was a quiet revolution at the turn of the century that protested the poor quality and monotony of goods produced by mechanization. Today at the turn of another century we have entered a new era of goods being produced by computer numerically controlled machinery. In the hope of saving our beleaguered crafts, we must establish a new paradigm in which crafts are accepted on an equal footing as fine art. Craftsmen, while we are mechanics, should also be included in the family of artists.

In our culture, marketing solid, enduring craftmanship, including the creativity and imagination that are a part of it, is an enormous challenge. We have a responsibility to encourage good taste and aesthetic responsibility in other disciplines around us including architecture, urban planning and development. Too much has been lost. It is important that we realize the vital role of handcrafts in our lives. . . .

Martin Ratermann,
Woodworker

. . . .Today, the role of the successful craftsman includes much more than applying skill. Marketing is now a large part of the equation in the survival of a craft business. Marketing on regional, national and international levels has made it possible for many Missouri artists to succeed.

We need to constantly strive to improve the visibility of the craft movement. Outreach organizations such as Best of Missouri Hands help to foster on the vital dialogue between new and established artists, so that they may continue to follow their dreams.

This book celebrates the integrity, creative spirit and artistic expressions of Missouri artists and craftsmen. . . .

Mary Benjamin,
Ceramic artist

Purpose Statement

The Missouri Artisans Business Development Association (MABDA) is a non-profit organization that provides creative and technical support for Missouri's art and craft community. The trademark for the organization is Best of Missouri Hands.

History of the Association

In 1985 the Home-Based Business Committee of the Alternatives for the 80s Project organized by the University of Missouri Extension founded the *Best of Missouri's Hands* project. This project was designed to provide marketing assistance for home-based Missouri artists.

The purpose was to increase family incomes in rural areas where changes in agriculture and manufacturing had resulted in the loss of many income opportunities. A retail craft catalog was designed to help them establish their businesses and become independent entrepreneurs.

High-quality artwork was identified through an intensive jurying process and in July 1986, Volume One of *Best of Missouri's Hands* was published. Worldwide distribution brought great success and national media attention in the *Wall Street Journal*, the *New York Times* and *Business Week*. Volume Two was published in 1988.

In 1989 this Home-Based Business Project spun off from the University forming the Missouri Artisans Business Development Association. This organization, with a solid foundation of accomplishment, continued to assist artists throughout the state with marketing, product development and business management assistance. Volumes Three and Four of *Best of Missouri's Hands* soon followed.

To address the educational needs of its members, Missouri Artisans Educational Foundation (MAEF) was formed. It sponsors marketing workshops and conferences throughout the state, as well as the annual statewide conference that attracts national speakers. All of these programs are open to the public.

The efforts of this organization have been highly successful in realizing the goals of the original project — new jobs, full-time businesses, increased incomes and as a result of the national and international exposure the artists and their work have been seen in over 100 publications.

Fourteen states now have programs as a result of Missouri's example. Group membership is open to all Missouri residents. For information on conferences and membership, see pages 126 and 127.

Making It All Happen

To accomplish its goals, the Missouri Artisans Business Development Association (MABDA) organizes and schedules educational conferences, produces a quarterly newsletter, offers access to selected wholesale trade shows and quality retail shows, offers information about outlets for products, developed a business expansion referral system and develops marketing tools to help market members' products.

    A. Annual conferences are held at a conveniently scheduled time and place to promote Association membership and assist artists with the details of marketing their products.

    B. A newsletter, developed by and distributed to members of the Association, provides timely information about new marketing opportunities and other business development tips useful for members.

    C. Group marketing opportunities for membership in wholesale trade shows, retail shows and advertising in state and national publications.

    D. A networking opportunity for artists which provides them access to other business development assistance. Examples of such assistance include business financing, employee training, design and development of business forms and brochures, record keeping, and other aspects of business development and management.

    E. Catalogs are developed, published and distributed by the Association. To date, four volumes of catalogs featuring the juried products of Missouri artists have been published. This effort serves to provide another source of income for the Association and provides extensive visibility for Missouri artists nationally and internationally.

    F. Creation and implementation of *Best of Missouri Hands: Profiles of the State's Fine Artists and Craftsmen.*

Ordering Information

The items in this book are either for sale as shown or are a representative sample of an artist's work. Many artists also accept commission work. Brochures and price lists are available on request from each artist.

Names, addresses and telephone numbers of artists are provided in the back of the book so that the buyer can contact them directly. Their work may appear in more than one category in the index.

Items listed in this book reflect retail prices. Wholesale buyers need to negotiate directly with each craftsman concerning price and the quantity that can be supplied. Many artists also accept phone and mail-order inquiries. Contact them directly for price lists or catalogs.

While every effort has been made to ensure the accuracy of information in this catalog, we cannot be responsible for errors in listing prices or other items.

Consult the listing of Missouri galleries at the back of the book for additional outlets for Best of Missouri products. Many artists also have mail-order catalogs.

*Profiles of the State's
Fine Artists and Craftsmen*

James Barksdale

JAMES BARKSDALE
Heritage Collection   *Jim Barksdale*

Specialty: High-quality, hand-carved one-of-a-kind shorebirds made from Missouri woods.
Media used: Basswood and sugar pine.
Price range: $30 to $150

The sounds of the ocean and shorebirds emanate from Willie Mole's Antique Shop in Steelville, the population center of the United States. Here, full-time hobbyist James Barksdale is busy freeing a bird form from a curved piece of sugar pine.

Small coastal shorebirds are the main carving interest for Jim. He researches his pieces by poring over volumes on decoys as well as bird identification books by Audubon and Roger Tory Peterson. Not only are his birds color correct, but historically correct as well.

Today his carvings serve as ornamental fixtures in homes, but they are modeled after hunting decoys that were used heavily in the 1800s up and down the East Coast, until the 1912 passing of the Migratory Bird Act.

Jim's lifelike seabird decoys authentically rekindle this bygone era. Sandpipers, avocets, yellowlegs, curlews, woodcocks and dowitchers are familiar decoys, painted in subdued hues of grey and tan. Jim also puts holes in his decoys, simulating the wear these decoys received.

James Barksdale

"These decoys were used to draw in the birds. The hunters actually shot the birds on the ground. So, the decoys got as many shot in 'em as the birds did," Jim said.

Jim carves both full-bodied birds and "flatties," which are thinner silhouettes of the birds, and were easier for hunters to carry and store.

In his Antique Series, Jim follows age-old traditions of using readily available materials in his decoys, such as tack eyes, cut-nail bills and distressed finishes. "Some have a nail for a beak... this one's got a bent gutter nail for a snout."

A unique krackled finish also gives carvings an aged patina. The acrylic series is to give a more realistic look to his carvings.

"I can do the same bird, the same pose, but they never turn out the same." Jim carved his first piece of wood some 40 years ago, but it wasn't until 15 years ago on a trip to Branson that he picked up the idea of carving shorebirds.

"That's always the first thing people ask, 'Are you from the coast?' Well, I've lived in Missouri all my life. I just really enjoy the shorebirds. There's such a variety. Everybody's doing ducks. I'm one of the very few who work with shorebirds. My pedestals of driftwood also really make mine stand out from those of other carvers.

"Antique shorebird decoys have become very collectable, with some selling for over $100,000 at auctions."

He cites *Best of Missouri's Hands* and several trade shows as the keys to building his hobby into a career. His work was also recently featured in *Midwest Living* magazine. His work is sold at Willie Mole's in Steelville and Bluestem Missouri Crafts in Columbia.

Marilyn Barnes

MARILYN BARNES
Adornments by Marilyn

Specialty: Originally designed, handcrafted Victorian-style jewelry designed from antique and vintage buttons, glass German cameos, replica brass pieces, porcelain hearts and roses, and Austrian crystals.
Media used: Antique buttons made of carved mother-of-pearl, pewter, brass, glass, cut steel, ivory and bone.
Price range: $6 to $39

Marilyn began designing antique buttons jewelry seven years ago when a combination of reasons seemed to come together all at the same time.

"I never gave very much thought to antique buttons, until a few years ago when my Mother gave me my Grandmother's old button box. I had no idea the attention to detail and miniature works of art that the buttons made during the golden age of button making (1860-1920) represent!"

Thus began an appreciation and interest which continues to grow.

"I have always had a deep interest in the elements of design, particularly the effect of the composition of three-dimensional items on each other, as well as the total outcome of the piece."

She graduated from Southwest Missouri State University with major emphasis in Interior Design and Art History, and her jewelry flows around collage-type designs.

Marilyn Barnes

"Believe it or not, there are actually a lot of design similarities between interior designing of rooms and designing of jewelry.

"The intricacies and painstaking attention to detail of buttons made in the 18th and 19th centuries fascinates us now because we are so accustomed to the mass produced look. The author Charles Dickens said of Victorian buttons, 'There is surely something charming in seeing the smallest thing done so thoroughly.' It is very interesting to trace the history of button making and how it reflects the changing fashions, art, society and industry of each era."

Most of the buttons Marilyn uses are from the mid-1800s to the early 1900s. She carefully searches for the best buttons made of glass, cut steel, brass, porcelain, enamel and mother-of-pearl. There is a limited supply and their value is constantly increasing.

The subjects depicted on Marilyn's antique buttons are quite diverse, including fables, opera themes, Greek mythology and innumerable drawings from animal and plant life.

"After I design a piece, I carefully research the buttons I use and record the dates they were made, materials and subject matter on the backs of the cards that go with each piece. My customers seem to really appreciate this interesting information. They realize they're getting a piece that is truly one-of-a-kind.

"I once read that success is 'Finding something that is worthwhile, that you love to do so much that you would do it for free, and then learning to do it so well that people will pay you to do it.' I feel blessed to say I have accomplished this."

Marilyn participates in about 20 art shows per year and supplies 12 shops with her jewelry. See her work at The Trader's Market and the Spring House at Galloway Village, both in Springfield, Mo.

Carole Behrer

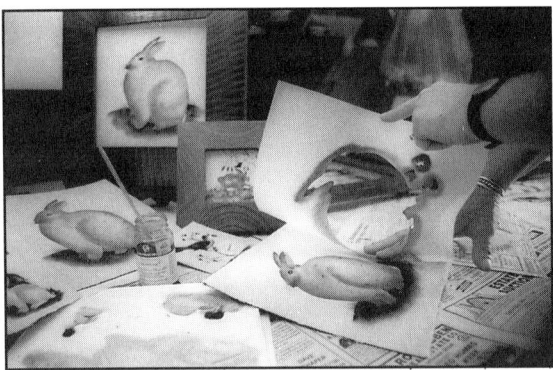

CAROLE BEHRER
Traditional Crafts

Specialty: Theorem painting (18th-century stenciling on white velvet) and *scherenschnitte* (German-style paper-cutting) framed in grain-painted frames. She also false grains furniture.

Media used: Pine frames, dried-pigment paint and beer, oil paint on white velvet dyed with tea, single sheets of paper for *scherenschnitte*.

Price range: $30 to $400

Carole Behrer

Carole Behrer has loved decorative folk art for most of her life. Her mother introduced Carole to the 18th-century art forms of *scherenschnitte*, theorem painting and grain-painting (false graining) after studying the original theorems at the Abby Aldrich Rockefeller Folk Art Museum in Williamsburg. She taught herself to reproduce them, and then taught Carole.

Today, Carole uses a refurbished chicken coop near her country home to create her own personal nest egg.

"I've been doing theorem painting for more than 12 years, and *scherenschnitte* for 13, reproducing many of the old patterns, and designing new work with the look of the old."

She frames both in grain-painted pine frames, so that the antique folk art look is complete. The false grain technique uses a combination of dry-pigment paint and beer applied with a feather and is then varnished.

Theorem painting, the art of painting designs on white velvet using stencils called theorems, was popular with ladies in finishing schools in the New England states from 1790 to 1850. After 1850, the availability of inexpensive Victorian floral prints relegated this art form to history.

Scherenschnitte, literally "scissors cutting" in German, was derived from the Swiss-German technique of cutting one piece of paper into a continuous design. The technique arrived in America in the late 18th century by way of birth certificates and love letters. Very small scissors are used to cut the paper, starting with cutting out all of the very small spaces first and progressing onto the larger cuts. The finished paper-cutting can also be watercolored for a different effect.

Her work is available at Old House in Hog Hollow in Chesterfield and the Firehouse Gallery in Eureka, Mo. She also sells her work through the Museum of American Folk Art in New York and the Abby Aldrich Rockefeller Folk Art Museum in Virginia. She was selected as one of *Early American Life* magazine's 200 best craftsmen for her work in theorem painting.

For the last 18 years, Carole and her husband John have lived at Shaw Arboretum in Gray Summit, Mo., where John is Superintendent.

Mary Benjamin

MARY BENJAMIN
Designs in Clay

Specialty: Jewelry — Necklaces, earrings and pins using a millefiore technique with colored clays.
Medium used: Porcelain.
Price range: $12 to $120

As Mary begins slicing and pressing multitudinous layers of clay together, she is awash with anticipation for what the clay will reveal.

By slicing lines and pressing different color clays on top of one another, she slowly forms the aquatic background for a fish.

"Oh look at this delicate line," she exclaims, revealing the clay's back side. "This is too good to pass up." And so she slices it and geometrically configures her next layer of clay, rolling it smooth again.

"This is a fascinating three-dimensional process. The structure and the surface are integral."

Mary is currently using the millefiore technique in clay. While most people think of porcelain as a pure white medium, she has added a new dimension with saturated colors.

"In the 80s, the widespread availability of commercial clay body stains

Mary Benjamin

gave me a suggestion for a new direction in my work. There are a few people using this technique for jewelrymaking, but I seem to have found my own approach."

She begins by kneading various metallic oxides — from persimmon to hazelnut, peacock to blackberry — into a pure white porcelain. Mary then stacks these color masses in various ways to build a multicolored loaf. When a cut is made down through the layers, a pattern emerges that is both singular and distinctive.

She then cuts these 12-inch layered loaves into cross sections. From these, she shapes her jewelry, sands and fires them and finally polishes each piece. These cross sections on a larger scale, are used for tiles and vessels. Mary is currently working on a series of wall reliefs and tile tables.

"This technique shows my love of pattern, derived mostly from the natural environment and from textiles of all sorts. The piecing of fabric in patchwork and how patterns are mixed continues to fascinate me. There is no end to this exploration."

When listening to her describe her jewelry, one sees a rebel gleam emerge. "It's a classic line that defies specific fashion styles. Every person who wears my work makes her own artistic statement."

Mary has been a studio potter for 20 years. She began working with clay in 1963, when she taught art at an elementary school in Honolulu, Hawaii. Today, she is one of five owners of Bluestem Missouri Crafts in Columbia, Mo.

"I work at Bluestem once a week. Art is such a solitary activity that it's beneficial to spend time with the people who respond to our work.

"When you are making a living with your art, very often your vocation and avocation are the same thing. It's hard for me to put it aside because I find such joy in what I do."

Her work is sold in Missouri at Bluestem Missouri Crafts in Columbia and Krueger Pottery in Webster Groves. She also sells her work in galleries nationwide at Signature Galleries in Massachusetts and Connecticut. Although jewelry is her major income, she often returns to the pottery that first got her started.

Steve Bland

STEVE BLAND
Aseity Kaleidoscopes

Specialty: Kaleidoscopes with pressed flowers.
Media used: Stained glass, pressed wildflowers, such as wild cyprus vine, Mexican heather, ageratum, verbena, lobelia and melampodium.
Price range: $32 to $170

    The move from human geneticist to creating kaleidoscopes full-time did not happen overnight. Five years ago, Steve realized he needed more control over his life and his schedule, so he founded Aseity Kaleidoscopes.
    "The name Aseity means *towards a state of self-existence*, exactly what this business represents for me."
    Today, Aseity offers seven different scope designs to shops around the country. Steve credits his success to knowing the materials he uses.

Steve Bland

"Others put four big flowers in their wheels. I use about twenty flowers with a wide variety of color and shapes. They really took off.

"I became a scope artist because I've worked in stained glass and have pressed flowers for years — and know how to press them well. I produce vibrant lasting colors and an interesting variety. I've found that many shops used to carry a floral scope but they sat on the shelf. I walk in with mine and they say, 'Oh my God, this one's different.' Here they find quality at a price they can afford."

Steve relies on a strong database and his developing business skills. "There is more to this than cutting glass. I spend a lot of time talking to shop owners and developing new markets.

"When people see me at shows and they have the full selection to choose from, by far my best seller is emerald green — but that wasn't the case last year. Keeping up with these trends, and passing that information on to my wholesale accounts is crucial," Steve said.

An early growth spurt from QVC, a television shopping network, showed Steve what was possible. "I produced in five weeks what took me nine months the year before. National coverage gave me a better sense of production capabilities. Now I'm not afraid of catalog or chain store orders."

Steve encourages others to follow their dreams. "A lot of people say they'd love to be living off of their talents, but that they feel stuck. My best advice is: wherever you are, start from there. If you have only five hours a week, start with that. It was a two-year transition for me, going just a little at a time. I was able to grow my business without stepping off the cliff. Many bosses are glad to have you part-time instead of losing you."

Steve wants to eventually run an artisans' incubator, helping others develop their creative talents into businesses. He is represented at Bluestem Missouri Crafts in Columbia, Mo., the Hanson Galleries in Houston, Texas, and Stardust by the Red Balloon in McClean, Virginia, among others.

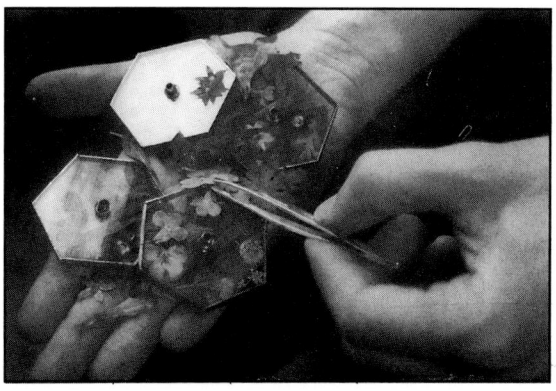

Serena Boschert

SERENA BOSCHERT
Hand-Painted Earthenware

Specialty: Hand-painted ceramic earthenware vases, art decor and Christmas ornaments. Specializing in custom hand-painted ornaments with portraits of home and pets.
Medium used: Earthenware clay.
Price Range: $5 to $500

St. Charles artist Serena Boschert relied on her past work experiences and her bachelor's and master's degrees in art to devote herself full-time to painting 15 years ago.

Her hand-casted earthenware becomes her canvas, resulting in her unique style — a combination of soft painting against the hard surface of the fired and glazed clay.

She was a charter member of MABDA, and her business risk paid

Serena Boschert

off. Her artwork has been featured in all four volumes of *Best of Missouri's Hands* catalogs and subsequently in *Glamour* and *Midwest Living* magazines, exposing her to a wide range of customers across the nation.

Staying disciplined and organized, Serena works from her home studio and sells at area art shows, through personal references and via mail orders. She is active in St. Louis area art activities and periodically teaches workshops and speaks at business seminars.

Although creating exquisite hand-painted vases, Serena says, "I've always been a Christmas person!" Only a few ornament designs are repeated, so variety keeps her work fresh. "I love creating. New designs are constantly in my mind and evolve into new ornaments every year."

Serena's ornaments range from small hand-created birdnests to elaborate jeweled balls that contain hand-painted scenes and figures — some even featuring hinged doors and lights.

Many ornaments become a sentimental reminder at Christmas of special events and memories of that year — a wedding, graduation, birthday, a child with a special toy or in a sports uniform. Homes (painted from a photograph) are featured in a snowscene setting. Pet portrait ornaments can feature the pet in a Christmas setting under the tree with Santa. This custom work is satisfying to her clients, and they appreciate the one-of-a-kind ornament that is unique and personal to them.

"Each ornament is a part of me," says Serena, "and it's a warm feeling to think of hundreds of my ornaments being opened on Christmas Day!"

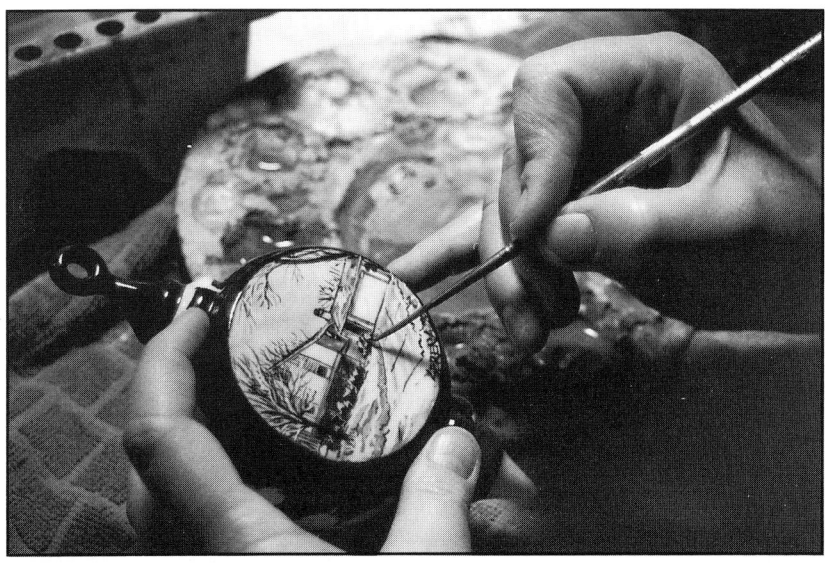

Carol Leigh Brack-Kaiser

CAROL LEIGH BRACK-KAISER
Carol Leigh's Specialties and **Hillcreek Fiber Studio**

Specialty: Teacher and retail supplier for weavers, spinners and natural dyers. She also sells unique triangle looms and does custom weaving.
Media used: Natural fibers and dyes.
Price range: $3 to $3,000. Products range from small gift items to major equipment and large tapestries.

Bright sunlight cascades upon richly colored skeins of yarns in Carol Leigh's studio, surrounding looms and other forms of fiber creation in a vibrant display of color. Carol Leigh Brack-Kaiser has been weaving, spinning and natural dyeing since 1979. She opened Carol Leigh's Specialties in 1982, specializing in natural fibers and dyes. She has done extensive research on the historic use of natural dyes in the Missouri Ozark region, and has written several articles on the subject.

"Nature provides fibers to clothe us and a glorious rainbow of colors. Being able to make useful items with our hands from products found in nature gives one a sense of self-fulfillment, satisfaction, independence, self-sufficiency and self-worth. A feeling not often found in today's fast-paced plastic society," Carol Leigh said.

Due to the demand from others to learn spinning, weaving and natural dyeing, she opened Hillcreek Fiber Studio in 1986. Carol Leigh teaches three spinning classes and two natural dye classes. She also teaches nu-

Carol Leigh Brack-Kaiser

merous felting and weaving classes. There is also an ongoing apprenticeship program established in 1986.

As her classes grew, students needed supplies, tools, equipment, more yarns than Carol Leigh could spin and books from which to learn. So the business continued to take on more dealerships in fiber-related products.

Carol Leigh's Specialties is now a retail shop carrying nearly everything spinners, weavers and natural dyers would need: spinning wheels and looms; 500 book and periodical titles; natural dyes from alkanet to zinc, including indigo, cochineal, madder root, safflower and two sizes of dye kits; many types of fibers to spin and yarns with which to weave or knit; and fiber-related gift items, including jewelry and note cards.

In addition to teaching, Carol Leigh and her son Carl developed the Spriggs Adjustable Triangle Loom. It adjusts to as large as seven feet. With the aid of her husband, Dennis, they sell more than 100 looms each year and ship them worldwide. This loom allows fast, easy weaving. By weaving and spreading loops apart, the warp and weft are from one continuous yarn, making color changes automatically symmetrical. The triangles are commonly fringed for shawls. Two or more triangles joined become blankets, bedcovers, ponchos, belted jackets and throw rugs.

Carol Leigh's Specialties is a family business with Dennis working long hours after his "other job," finishing and packaging looms, doing bookwork and helping wherever needed. Her son Carl creates numerous wood products for spinning and weaving, including Triangle, Navajo and Inkle Looms and Spindles, daughter Rebecca helps with merchandizing, daughter Rose teaches finger-weaving and helps package products, and ex-husband Phil does computer work and record-keeping.

For a current product catalog or for directions to the studio, contact Carol Leigh directly, and please call before coming out. Carol Leigh is a charter member of MABDA and has been in all four *Best of Missouri's Hands* volumes and can be found demonstrating at many rendezvous and historical events.

Rick & Sue Braun

RICK & SUE BRAUN
Wood Merchant

Specialty: Custom-designed, quality driftwood furniture and installation pieces, residential and commercial, from indigenous and other domestic solid wood. Each piece is signed and dated.
Media used: Woods including cherry, walnut, sycamore, redwood, maple burl, manzanita and oak, glass, metal and stone.
Price range: $20 to $10,000

Maple burl grains in a table top show eons of slow growth. Now the wood slab sits polished to the light of appreciation squarely upon a driftwood base.

"Seeing all this natural beauty just sitting there and usually rotting away, unappreciated, became the focus for starting our business," Rick said, whose company highlights Nature's one-of-a-kind creations by turning neglected driftwood into furnishing focal points.

"We are at the whim of Mother Nature for our raw materials. My fascination with wood began as a child in Wisconsin. Walks in the woods and along shore lines always piqued my imagination.

Rick & Sue Braun

"Mother Nature gets the credit for the basis of all my designs. The shape, color, intricacies (in-grown rocks, matted roots and unique forms) are already there. I just have the ability to see this beauty and turn it into creations that 'speak' to everyone, and can be enjoyed and appreciated now and for generations to come.

"Since opening in 1980, our business and clientele have grown extensively. Our greatest satisfaction comes from creating the highest quality work that's appreciated by collectors all over the United States."

Their big break came early on. "The owner of Bass Pro Shop's Dogwood Canyon resort came by my shop one day and asked if I'd be interested in building more furniture like this. Two days later his architect came down, and well, they just kept ordering and ordering."

In Missouri their work can be seen at Big Cedar Lodge Resort. Their main lodge is on Table Rock Lake at 612 Devil's Pool Road in Ridgedale, Missouri. Although this is not a retail outlet for the Brauns' work, all of the main lodge and their cabins are furnished by Wood Merchant.

Rick and Sue's shop has since moved near Blue Eye, into an old lumber company building that gives Rick room to work on multiple projects and house more equipment. Rick and Sue are equally comfortable putting the finishing touches on designer log cabins and searching the coves of Missouri lakes in his V-bottom boat.

"I take my boat and a map and just start searching the coves for pieces that will work for me. I collect only downed, dead wood. I'm not always sure when I pick it up what would be the best use, so I store it.

"From collecting the driftwood to the final finish and the numerous processes in between, there is great satisfaction and pride in creating a piece that you hope will bring an awareness of the splendid beauty and character that only Mother Nature can provide."

Most work is done on a custom basis. Rick says it's this uniqueness that customers can't get anywhere else.

The Brauns often visit their customers' homes to give them suggestions.

"I'm the brains and he's the Braun," Sue said.

"And if I don't have what they're looking for," Rick said, "I get back in the boat and start looking."

Vickie Canham

VICKIE CANHAM
Aesthetic Arts Studio

Specialty: Fine porcelain giftware, portraits, Christmas ornaments and custom ceramic tile.
Media used: Porcelain and ceramic tile.
Price range: $10 to $2,250. Prices vary per commission.

Whether on porcelain or canvas, Vickie's goal has always been to translate the emotion of the soul into a visual reality, creating something of beauty that all can enjoy. Her dream of sharing her art with others was realized with the creation of Aesthetic Arts Studio.

"I love porcelain — its history, quality and the techniques involved in painting different styles," Vickie said. "I mix my paint from powder by grinding and mixing them with various oils — just like the old masters.

"There is a wonderful satisfaction that comes from continuing art

Vickie Canham

traditions that are hundreds and even thousands of years old."

On canvas she enjoys painting landscapes, garden scenes and Celtic designs. On porcelain, she specializes in hand-painted portraits including miniatures. Her museum-quality porcelain includes work with raised gold and enamel, traditional fruits, florals, birds and landscapes, along with many different internationally known styles of paintings.

Vickie has painted with and learned from many porcelain artists from across America, along with artists from Europe, South America and the Orient.

A client can choose to have a piece commissioned and painted on anything from Limoges boxes, vases, trays, jewelry pendants, Christmas ornaments, and porcelain tiles ready for framing.

Vickie has transferred her experience and expertise in painting porcelain into painting on ceramic tiles. She paints custom ceramic tiles for the kitchen, bath or fireplace, along with hand-painted sinks and accessories. Glass lamps can also be painted to match a client's tile or decor. Her fired-on process creates a permanent bond between the paint and the glaze.

"There are many home decorators who pore over catalogs looking for the right wall and floor coverings. They end up frustrated and settle for something less than what they desired. I specialize in bringing their expectations into reality."

Vickie says her greatest joy in working with clients is the design process. Vickie works to create a custom look that is an extension of themselves and the home they wish to create.

Vickie's work has appeared in the *China Decorator* and the *British Porcelain Artist*. She has also been a guest speaker at several events, speaking on such topics as marketing art and home-based businesses.

"The art I create comes from within, from the very essence of who I am, and is designed to produce an emotional and sensory response through a visual image," she said.

Her work can be seen at Tucker's Fine Jewelry & Gift Gallery in Columbia, Mo.

Bruce & Cathy Clemens

BRUCE & CATHY CLEMENS
Silver Feather Jewelry

Specialty: Jewelry based on feather designs and Native American themes.
Media used: Sterling silver and copper married metals.
Price range: $20 to $150

    Cathy and Bruce Clemens are full-time silversmiths working from their studio in Galena. Their work features feathers as a theme, and takes its inspiration from the rich imagery and the spiritual tradition of Native American culture.
    Five years ago, they left the bustle of their careers in California to pursue artistic passions full-time in Missouri.
    "My parents moved here to retire. They told us about this house for sale and we bought it sight unseen," Bruce said. Now, the 100-foot commute between home and shop replaces the six-lane traffic jams of the West Coast.
    Each of their pieces is hand-fabricated using unique "married metals" processes that combine sterling silver and copper to create an elegant item with the beauty of silver enriched by the warmth of copper.

Bruce & Cathy Clemens

"My work draws its inspiration from the rich and meaningful imagery of the Plains Indians culture which reveres the feathers of the eagle and other raptors as the carriers of prayers and views those animals as intercessors between people's earthly lives and a more spiritual, heavenly realm.

"The hoops and medicine wheels I use throughout my designs represent the circle of all life on the planet and remind us that we are all part of the greater whole and not to separate ourselves from our proper place in nature and the family of the Great Spirit."

Cathy has a master's of Fine Arts degree from Claremont Graduate School and has experience in ceramics, printmaking, woodworking and graphic arts. She and Bruce began working in silver in 1985 and soon made married-metal feature pieces their specialty.

Their line has developed into a distinctive and unusual collection of earrings, pins, bracelets and pendants that have achieved acclaim for artistic merit and quality throughout the United States and in Japan and Germany.

Cathy and Bruce are also founding members of the Southwest Missouri Craft Guild. Their work is in the collections of such notables as Andy Williams, Ralph Lauren, Willie Nelson, Johnny Cash, Bonnie Raitt and thousands of people they meet as they pursue their rigorous show schedule each season.

When they're not working on their product lines, Cathy works on untraditional contemporary jewelry pieces for fun. Bruce creates fine folding knives as a hobby and is currently also studying clock-making with the prestigious British Horological Institute.

Their work can be seen at galleries throughout Missouri, including Cornerstone Fine Metals at Silver Dollar City in Branson; the Springfield Art Museum Gift Shop, the Showcase Galleries and at Renaissance Books & Gifts, all in Springfield.

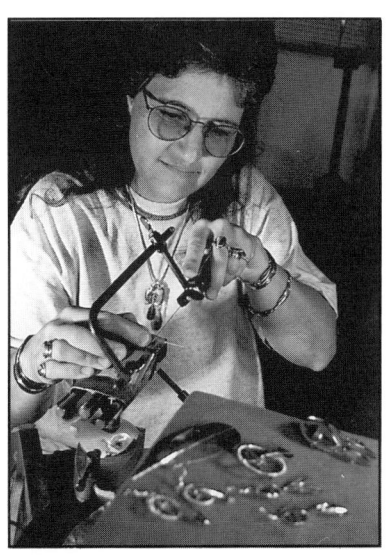

Connie Copley

CONNIE COPLEY
The Con Artist

Specialty: Unique one-of-a-kind jewelry designed from vintage and contemporary findings.
Media used: Found objects, antique cast-offs, vintage beads, contemporary charms and semi-precious stones.
Price range: $25 to $125

"At the heart of my work is a belief — not in what is — but in what can be," Connie said. "In my studio, cut steel shoe buckles, vintage dress ornaments and tarnished streetcar tokens integrate with glass beads, Austrian crystals or semi-precious stones to become unexpected pieces of jewelry. A handful of 1930 bakelite poker chips receives new life as bracelet trinkets when combined with game dice and African trade beads."

Connie Copley

As with most people pursuing artistic endeavors, Connie draws satisfaction both from finding her materials and in making them into something new.

"My work reflects my diligent search for unusual findings in antique shops and private collections across the country."

Beauty in the commonplace is the thread that ties her work together. Glass rings from a San Francisco artist, old clock keys from the Michigan flea market and steel cut buttons from Grandmother's sewing basket find a new home on her work table.

"My whimsical style sometimes mixes the old with the new. Contemporary hearts and stars mesh with trinkets from the 1920s while 60s' peace signs reappear with Victorian baubles. Each piece is an original, one-of-a-kind creation utilizing past relics and found objects meticulously made with love and imagination."

Her work can be seen at The Greeting Gallery in Clayton, Mo.

Ann Crume

ANN CRUME
Paper Chase

Specialty: Papermaking kits and handmade paper created from junk mail and other recyclables.
Media used: Junk mail and paper headed for the trash.
Price range: Kits range from $9.25 to $30. Paper ranges from $2.75 to $10.

Ann's interest in papermaking began in 1992. A newspaper article described a papermaker selling her handmade paper through Niemann Marcus.

"I was intrigued," Ann said. "While experimenting with papermaking, I discovered a process for making paper from junk mail. I love it!

"With a background in medical records and office management, I simply felt like I was going from one type of paper handling to another," Ann says of her career change. "I have always enjoyed learning new things, especially if it's a challenge. Papermaking certainly fulfills that criteria, researching and experimenting with various methods and techniques.

"Sharing papermaking with others is exciting. So many people are interested in the recycled papermaking process, that I developed papermaking kits. I made certain the process was simple (those from ages 4 to 80 are using the kits) and following the exact way I make recycled paper in my kitchen."

Kits include instructions, the mold and deckle (which is the sheet papermaker) and *couching* supplies. Making recycled handmade paper is an easy step-by-step process: Collect junk mail. (No problem.) Sort by color. Tear into small pieces. Blend in a kitchen blender with water. Shape into sheets or cast paper-art creations. Then let the paper dry.

"Prior to finishing a sheet of paper or a paper casting I anticipate the outcome. Most are really good and a few go back into the blender."

Ann uses the sheets for stationery and notes. Handmade sheet paper can also be embellished by embossing, adding herbs, leaves and flowers.

"When using my ceramic molds, a person can create ornaments that decorate gift boxes, baskets, wreaths and cards. They can be painted with watercolor, acrylic, pastels, crayons and cosmetics.

"When anyone asks me, 'What do you do?' and I reply 'I make paper from junk mail' it's a great opportunity to tell them about handmade paper. Meeting and teaching wonderful people has been a fantastic reward."

Ann is eager to share her enthusiasm, "The Chinese developed papermaking in 105 A.D. The Europeans were making paper as early as the 12th century. As the Europeans came to the New World they brought papermaking with them.

"When you dip your first sheet of paper, you will join a centuries-old group of craftspeople. Have fun and recycle too!"

Ann sells her papermaking kits through her mail-order catalog. Contact her directly for information on kits, presentations and demonstrations for groups.

Ann's kits are available in Missouri at Exclusively Missouri in Lee's Summit, I'd Rather Be Stamping in Columbia, Homestead's in Liberty and the Missouri Botanical Gardens in St. Louis.

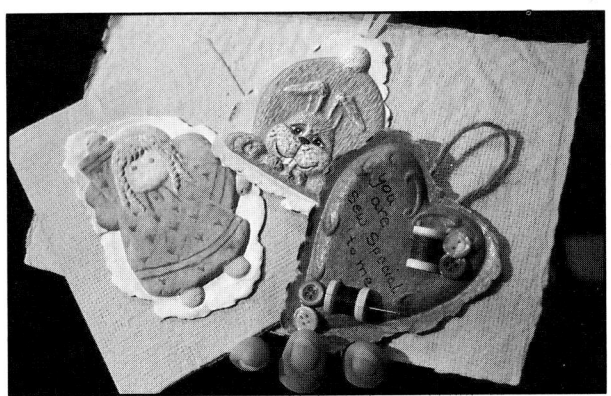

Diana Denman

DIANA DENMAN
Wolf's Point Studio

Specialty: Wheel-thrown and slab-built functional and decorative stoneware, fused glass and blown glass ornaments, flutes and jewelry.
Media used: Stoneware, clay (Raku and porcelain), gemstones, silver, gold, glass beads, borasilicate glass, blown and lampworked, and fused art glass.
Price range: $2 to $75. Commission work accepted.

Diana creates with both clay and glass. Instead of viewing them as separate art forms, she sees their elemental silica structure as the real medium, which she seeks to transform into functional works of art.

"Fire tranforms silica into a new creation," Diana said. "It's infinite in its possibilities. I never feel bored, because you can do about anything with it. I create artful items for daily life."

From Wolf's Point Studio, established in 1978, Diana creates wheel-thrown and slab-built stoneware, imprinted with nature's textures.

"When I press fabric and plant material into the clay, I feel like I'm creating fossils. I love the texture and the color of inlaid oxides."

Inspired by the delicate beauty of inherited family lace, Diana began to use lace and plant impressions to create larger free-form bowls, trays

Diana Denman

and wallpockets, sometimes combining the slabs with thrown bases.

"I find myself continually inspired by the clay and glaze and oxides as they fire to become things of beauty. I knew at age 19 that I wanted to work in clay and glass. Ever since I've had a chance to make a decision in my life, I've chosen life as an artist. I thank God for blessing me with the gift of creativity."

Diana began studying pottery with Mary Benjamin at the Columbia Art League in 1973. She then took classes, group and private, at the MSA Craft Studio with John Preus and Anita Salizar and attended workshops with Shel Nemark and other accomplished potters.

"I eventually studied at Stephens College with Ralph Komovis, Sue Luger and Lori Sargent. As I became more accomplished with my throwing, I continued refining my techniques for handbuilding slab forms.

"My studio in Lupus (population 28) on the Missouri River is good fodder for the creative process. By the grace of God and the help of a lot of friends we have survived two major floods. We have plans to elevate the studio above future flooding."

In addition to pottery, Diana has worked with fused glass for several years, mostly making jewelry. "There are a lot of similarities with clay. The circular motion of working the heated glass, the wheel work . . . it's all centered around the core . . . it's the same."

Diana also spent nine years as a University of Missouri scientific glassblower. Now she works with the borasilicate glass seasonally, making blown and lampworked ornaments and glass flutes.

Her work can be seen at the Columbia Art League and Mythmaker Galleries, both in Columbia. Other Missouri galleries include The Classic Touch in Fulton, the High Gate Gallery in Rocheport, the House of Mary B in Arrow Rock, Clan Vital Studios in Jefferson City, and The Moniteau Trader in Jamestown.

Dodie Eisenhauer

DODIE EISENHAUER
Village Designs

Specialty: Wire-mesh angels, bows, ornaments and vine trees.
Media used: Screen wire and wire.
Price range: $5 to $125

Dodie Eisenhauer, creator of wire-mesh designs, has been an artist for 25 years in the rural town of Daisy. "Don't blink when you drive through," says Dodie. "We have a sign one side of town and another one on the other side of town, and they're almost back-to-back," she continues, laughing. Though a native of Daisy, Dodie had moved 17 times with her military husband before settling their family of seven back in Daisy.

Twenty-seven years ago, one of those relocations landed Dodie in the Missouri Ozarks, where she began free-handing designs on tinware. Then she began painting on lap desks and thimbles. Dodie enjoyed local marketing and craft shows, but the income was sporadic.

The idea of designing with wire mesh was dropped into Dodie's artistic spirit early one morning after attempting to rescreen her grandmother's old door. The door was soon pushed aside as the creative process began, turning the wire mesh into bows, baskets and eventually, angels.

Against the advice of her friends, Dodie responded to an article about *Best of Missouri's Hands*. "Little did I know how it would change my life," says Dodie, now the owner of Village Designs. Today her work ap-

Dodie Eisenhauer

pears in Missouri at Exclusively Missouri and Sebree Galleries. Nationwide, her distribution includes the Museum of American Folk Art and Bergdorf Goodman in New York and Gumps in San Francisco.

"Since the road kind of ends here, those semi's picking up our shipments sometimes have to back up to the highway to turn around."

One day she works with miniature angels, the next day she's crating up nine-foot bows to adorn the front of a department store. Now she employs 20 people and many members of her family. Besides her husband who cuts all the wire pieces for the angels, her 88-year-old father makes all the halos.

Dodie was catapulted into the national scene via wholesale trade shows, where she met her marketing rep and established the idea for her most popular item to date: wire-mesh angels.

"This group made me aware that I could tap into different avenues of marketing other than just craft shows. Without this group, I wouldn't have gotten into the wholesale market. I wouldn't have gone nationwide."

Despite riding the crest of her burgeoning business, Dodie still maintains a good perspective. "I still feel my home is my priority. Being a Mom and a wife is the most important thing.

"I feel this is God's will to have me here doing this. This is about more than just business. This is about helping other mothers to work at home so they can be with their family. My family is my biggest supporter and biggest critic. I was at this for four years before I was allowed to hang one of my angels on our Christmas tree," she said.

Jewel & William Ernst

JEWEL & WILLIAM ERNST
Loutre Valley Enterprises

Specialty: Basketry, caning, woodworking and framing.
Media used: Reeds, canes, splints and wood.
Price range: $15 to $70 (more for some frames).

Like the Native Americans before them, Heartland pioneers fashioned baskets from materials they gathered on the prairies and in the woodlands: sweet grass, rye straw, young willow and splints from oak, ash and hickory trees. With skilled hands they wove twined and coiled lightweight containers.

Today, the Ernsts' collection pays homage to the beauty and tradition of Midwest basket-making. Each basket is handcrafted, using essentially the same centuries-old methods their ancestors did.

Jewel Ernst started out learning a craft to fill a little time as she edged into semi-retirement. She enrolled in a basket-making class. Then her husband Bill joined her and they learned the craft together. Eventually Bill turned the focus of his talent into other areas such as making cane woven chair seats and stools.

Jewel, on the other hand, focused on making baskets.

" It's just one of those things I need to do. What else can I say?"

Her talents have won her accolades at state shows and fairs. Those honors brought her some more business and perhaps an even bigger honor, being featured in *Midwest Living* magazine.

Jewel sells all the baskets she makes or gives them as gifts. "I make many reproductions of old-fashioned baskets — egg baskets, hearth baskets and feather baskets, but I also have some original designs."

Jewel keeps samples of the different kinds of baskets in their country home two and a half miles south of Mineola. She enjoys using innovative ideas of interweaving colors and textures in her baskets. "A customer can look over the variety, make a selection and I'll make their basket to order or they can buy a basket I've already made."

Jewel and Bill Ernst are also charter members of Missouri Artisans Business Development Association.

Peggy Feagins

PEGGY FEAGINS
OakLeaf Pottery

Specialty: Functional, hand-thrown stoneware pottery.
Media used: Clay and lead-free glazes.
Price range: $7.50 to $250

Peggy first made pottery as a child when her grandmother helped her dig and prepare clay from the old family homestead in Minnesota. From this, she made little cups and saucers, plates and bowls for her dolls.

Years later during a trip to Arizona she watched a Hopi potter work, and decided to revive her own long-lost interest. "I got so excited," Peggy remembers, "watching her work with the clay, I could hardly wait to try it again myself." Back in Missouri, she got some clay and began hand-building, then took a class in wheel-thrown pottery. She was hooked. "I started to sell by word of mouth, then through art fairs, then in the *Best of Missouri's Hands* catalog."

Working out of her Grandview basement, Peggy jokingly calls herself an "underground artist." Here she produces her "domestic ware" — functional stoneware, meant to be used and enjoyed every day. One of her specialties is colanders that she creates in a variety of shapes and sizes. These are handy for rinsing and serving fruits, vegetables and pasta.

Peggy also makes vases, canisters, lamps, clocks, dish sets and more. "One of the things I love about clay is its impressionability, and I like to

Peggy Feagins

make use of plants in decorating my work." Among others, oak leaves, cedar, wheat and Queen Anne's lace leave their impressions on many of her pots.

Having recently become a grandmother herself and remembering the pleasures of those little dishes formed in her childhood, Peggy designed a set of small dishes for her granddaughter. This has led to the creation of a new product, "Keepsake Dishes" — a line of miniature dishes for children and collectors. The miniatures, like the rest of her pottery, are handmade, ovenproof, microwave and dishwasher safe, and lead-free.

"It's great to be in business doing something you love," Peggy admits. "I love the clay, I love well-made pots, and it is a delight to know my pottery is being used and enjoyed in homes around the country and beyond."

"I believe art is a reflection of our values, of what's important to us," Peggy said. "For me, family and home are top priorities. I hope my pottery reflects that."

Her work can be seen at the Kansas Sampler Stores in the Kansas City area and at the State Fare store in Union Station, St. Louis. Her work is also available through mail-order catologs and at regional art shows.

Lee & Pam Ferber

LEE & PAM FERBER
Peola Valley Pottery

Specialty: Handmade stoneware pottery, earthenware Christmas ornaments and ceramic jewelry.
Medium used: Clay.
Price range: $3 to $300

Deep within the Ozark hills near the Black River lies Peola Valley Pottery. Lee and Pam Ferber happened upon these secluded environs while taking the backroads on a trip from Iowa to Mississippi. Of their flight to country living, one friend joked that it was the world's most carefully thought out mid-life crisis.

Yet the Ferbers found a lifestyle very different than what they expected from reading the Whole Earth Catalogs and Mother Earth News.

"We planted a very large garden figuring our first years would be pretty lean. But the first day we opened, we sold $300. We turned to retailing due to the untapped tourist market around these wilderness retreats."

Prior to this commitment to full-time pottery, Lee was associated with the Art Department at Drake University for 17 years. Peola Valley Pottery was founded in 1984. In 1989, the pottery opened the Peola Valley Store, a gallery to showcase their work as well as other high-quality handmade Missouri products.

Lee's customized coffee mugs have been such a hit, orders now keep him busy year-round. Lee started making coffee cups as a fund-raiser for Scouts. Then a friend ordered 1,000 cups, and his business began to grow.

"Our custom stoneware mugs have been made for business promotions, family reunions, church groups, bed and breakfasts, and as Christmas gifts," Lee said. "I've probably made 10,000 to 12,000 coffee cups — but never more than 20 a day. I still like starting with a lump of clay and working it into something more. We make a custom die for each customer, so these are truly unique. The mugs are finished in dark blue or teal green."

Lee says many customers over the years have asked in a roundabout way "don't you miss making art?"

Lee is very comfortable with his transition into a second career. "In my previous life as a professor, I had a piece accepted into the Smithsonian permanent display and played that whole game, but I never made a penny. You can't make a living making exhibition pieces. Here I've been able to start a business and have it succeed. That's very rewarding. I like the rewards of doing everything myself."

Their store is open from 9 a.m. to 4 p.m. every day but Monday. Visitors during the off season (December through March) are encouraged to call to confirm store hours. Visitors are welcome to visit the studios and observe work in progress.

Peola Valley Store is located three miles south of Highway 21, near Lesterville, on Peola Road. The pottery is located within a short drive of the highest point in Missouri, Taum Sauk Mountain. Also close by are the Johnson's Shut-Ins State Park, Elephant Rocks State Park and Fort Davidson State Park and Museum.

Visitors to the pottery that need overnight accomodations should contact Wilderness Lodge at (573) 637-2295. Arrangements for canoe rentals can also be made at this number.

Peola Valley pottery is also available at Bluestem Missouri Crafts in Columbia and at Krugers Pottery in St. Louis.

Jeannette Fischer

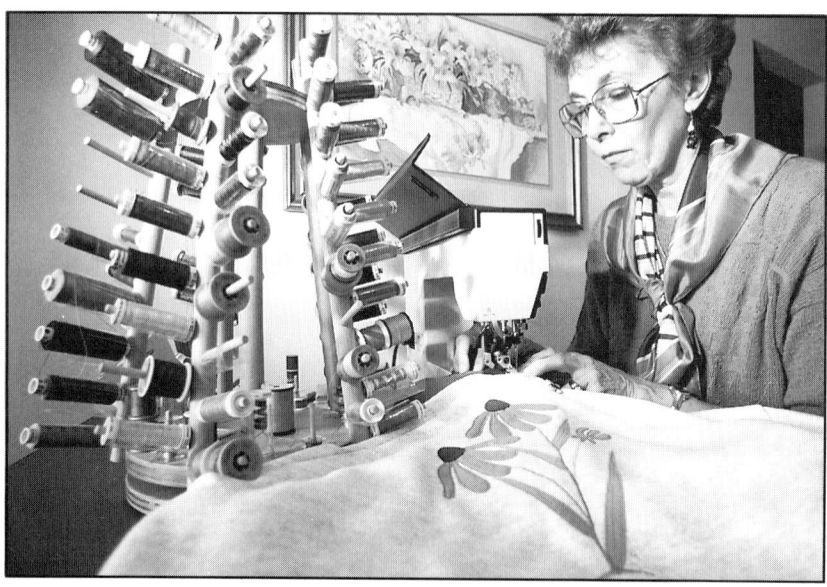

JEANNETTE FISCHER
Designs by Jeannette

Specialty: Applique sweatshirts.
Media used: Variety of fibers, handmade buttons, antique beads.
Price range: $28 to $45

Jeannette's love of fabrics began when she was a small child as she helped her mother mix and match feedsack prints for quiltmaking. Her mother was an avid quiltmaker, so Jeannette was exposed at an early age to the artistic blending of colors and prints.

"My first experience with quality fabrics occurred when I was about six years old and received a pair of hand-me-down red silk pajamas. I have loved red, silk and quality fabrics since that first encounter."

The applique embellishments that Jeanette uses include quality cottons, Ultra Suede, handmade buttons and antique beads. These mediums all come together from her home in the upper Ozarks, nestled in an oak forest. From her window she enjoys whitetail deer, wild turkeys and occasionally a pair of pileated woodpeckers. In this quiet, peaceful setting, her compositions take form.

And perhaps it is because of these surroundings that she was inspired to develop a series of Missouri wildflower designs. Purple coneflowers and dogwood are two of her favorites. And with ongoing research and inspiration, the list of varieties continues to bloom and grow.

Mary Frazier

MARY FRAZIER
Ancient Images

Specialty: Gourds rendered and aged in various media.
Media used: Missouri-grown gourds, acrylic paints, stains and dyes. Embellished with natural materials.
Price range: $40 and up.

With an artistic vision in mind, gourd artist Mary Frazier carefully selects hard-shelled gourds according to size, shape and type from growers in southwest Missouri. The dried, sometimes moldy and dirty gourds must then be scrubbed clean and scraped, removing any remnants of skin to reveal the wonderful wood-like working surface. Many hours later, the end result is a beautiful original artwork.

Gourds are believed to have originated in Africa and found their way to all corners of the earth by floating across oceans. Gourds have been used for ceremonial and utilitarian purposes for centuries and have been found throughout the world in graves, tombs, caves and ancient ruins. Evidence shows that the Eastern Woodland Indians cultivated gourds as early as 1000 B.C. using them as drinking cups, bowls, fishing floats, rattles, eating utensils, storage containers and musical instruments. In some parts of the world gourds were even used as currency. In the past few years there has been a renewed interest in gourds as an art medium and many artists are using a variety of ways to create fine art from dried gourds of all kinds.

Mary Frazier

With her background as an oil painter for over 20 years, Mary happened onto some hundred-year-old gourds in a Texas museum and immediately saw an exciting new medium.

"After a year of researching and learning about growing, drying and decorating, a reliable source for dried gourds was located making it possible to begin painting, staining, dyeing, carving and embellishing," Mary said.

While living in the Southwest several years ago, Mary became interested in the design elements on pottery artifacts found there and discovered that certain types of gourds were the perfect medium to create her own original "ancient" designs. Mary's pots often look like they have just been dug from the earth. Since gourds are a natural product, there are no two alike with each design created for a particular gourd. In addition to the artifact gourds, Mary also designs elegant gourd folk art Santas, and a variety of other figure gourds, continually developing new ideas. All gourds are signed by the artist and display the Best of Missouri Hands logo.

Mary's work has been juried into the fall 1996 show at the Emerson Art and Cultural Center in Bozeman, Montana, and she will exhibit at Out of Your Gourd 1996 in Santa Fe, New Mexico. Mary is a member of the American Gourd Society.

Fine art gourds from Ancient Images can be seen at Tan Tara Resort, Lake of the Ozarks, Wood'n Ya Want It Gallery in Osage Beach, and Bluestem Missouri Crafts in Columbia, Mo.

Meg Gibson

MEG GIBSON
Gibson Glass Bead

Specialty: Lampworked glass. Specializing in one-of-a-kind jewelry.
Media used: Glass and sterling silver.
Price range: $3 to $210

As the glass glows molten red, Meg slowly revolves the beginnings of a bead to keep it round and defy gravity's pull. She touches it with another glass rod and a tear-shaped blob breaks away onto the surface of the bead. As she continues to rotate and heat the mix, the blob and bead absorb into one another and she moves on to the next dot.

"You can go on adding dots almost indefinitely," Meg said.

Meg's jewelry is whimsical yet elegant, including metallic dichroic designs, polka-dot glass beads, hearts and crazy one-of-a-kinds. She also sells individual beads for those wishing to create their own masterpieces.

Meg met a fused-glass artist in Moscow, Idaho, who taught her how to melt glass over a flame onto a metal rod — a process known as lampworking.

"I fell in love with these little glass orbs. Being a person who thrives on immediate gratification, and a closet pyromaniac, I've found the perfect art form. I'm totally addicted," Meg said.

"Add colors . . . change shapes . . . smoosh . . . squash and moments

Meg Gibson

later I have my finished piece. Letting it cool for two hours without peeking is often excruciating.

"Patterns emerge and I am often looking at something I hadn't originally planned or even dreamed about. It's those surprises I love.

"What I find even more exciting is how all those tiny parts or beads fit together to create the whole — the finished necklace."

Glass is a growing artistic medium in this country. Just 10 to 15 years ago, there were "maybe three glass beadmakers in this country. Now there are probably two or three thousand," Meg said.

Because of this growth, there is more knowledge, equipment, supplies and support networks available. Meg is a member of the Society of Glass Beadmakers.

"Glass is a mystery. One that intrigues young and old alike," she said. "I feel as if I have just skimmed the surface of the possibilities. I have so much to look forward to."

Her work is available at Bluestem Missouri Crafts in Columbia, Mo., as well as the Vespermann Gallery in Atlanta, Kittrell-Riffkind Art Glass in Dallas, and galleries in California and Colorado.

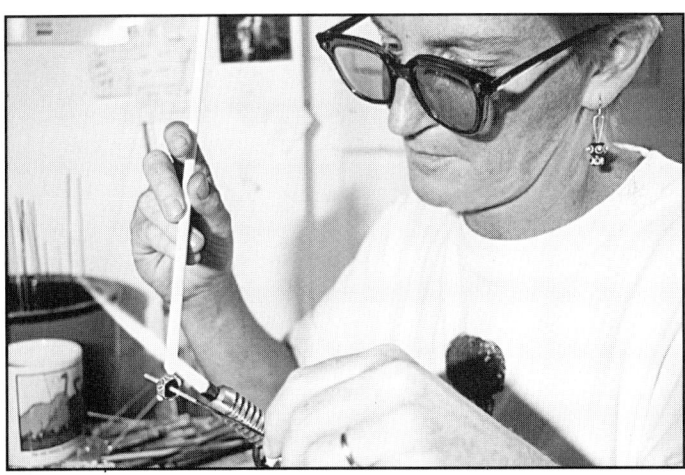

Steve Gorman

STEVE GORMAN
Painted Sculptures

Specialty: Three-dimensional paintings and painted sculptures.
Media used: Clay and acrylic, ceramic stains.
Price range: $30 to $4,000

Growing up in the Kansas City area, Steve has been an artist for as long as he can remember. One of his favorite memories is learning to draw in his grandma's kitchen on the old enamel-topped table.

Steve's sculptures are made of earthenware clay. Each piece is made using the slab and/or pinch method, in which carving, smoothing and refining of the surface may take several hours after the initial form has been completed. After the bisque-firing and more surface refinement, the work is finally ready for color, which is applied with an airbrush. Because of his compulsion for quality, a large piece may take 40 or 50 hours from conception to completion, with days spent sanding each piece to its smooth finish.

In his quest to grow as an artist, Steve has experimented with several different media including pencil drawing, watercolor, oil, acrylic and wall reliefs built with wood, plaster and painted with oil.

"My work just kept screaming to come off the canvas. I worked with textures, layering and finally moved to pottery. Now, every side, every curve, offers a unique perspective of the piece."

Coming to the conclusion that he is a painter that also loves to sculpt, Steve has begun creating three-dimensional paintings and painted sculptures.

"Over the years, I have searched for the medium that best expresses my ideas of form, color, simplicity and movement in one visual statement," he said. "As a result, I have executed a series of painted, abstract, organic clay pieces combining the mediums of painting and sculpture. Drawing and spontaneous interaction with the clay are two methods that I use to achieve a final sculptural form."

After firing, a double action airbrush is used to achieve the smooth blending of color on each piece.

Color selection and using an airbrush for soft delicate gradient completes the process. Observers have remarked that the harmony between form and color often creates a feeling of serenity.

Steve has been exhibiting in festivals throughout the Midwest this year and in the past several months has had pieces accepted into eight national and international museum exhibits.

Steve has also taught art in the public schools since 1985, most recently at Winnetonka High School in North Kansas City.

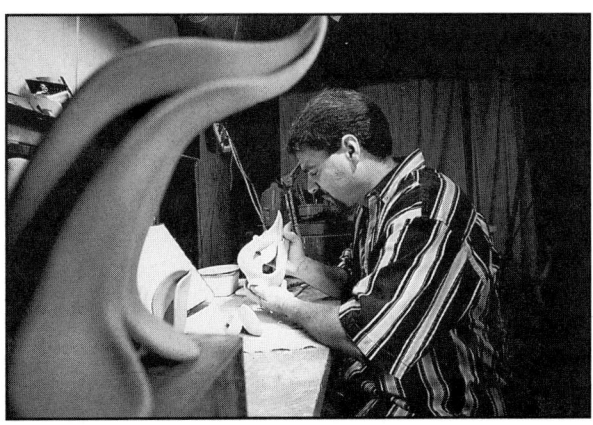

Grette Herrick

GRETTE HERRICK
Old Courthouse Studio and Gallery

Specialty: Wildflowers.
Media used: Although she is accomplished in ink, colored pencil and acrylic, Grette Herrick's favorite medium is watercolor.
Price range: $50 to $500

Grette Herrick's favorite medium is watercolor, but she is also accomplished in ink, color pencil and acrylic. She has been drawing and painting ever since she can remember.

Although she paints landscapes, still lifes and portraits, her favorite subjects are wildflowers. These she paints live, in watercolor, faithfully reproducing colors and features.

Recalling that her mother and grandmother gathered many of the wildflowers and plants she paints today, Grette began to sample the wild-

Grette Herrick

ings herself. She nibbles violets, spiderwort, sorrel and rose petals while in the field and enjoys cooking with them.

She wanted to share her wonderful discoveries with others, so her notecards and bookmarks entitled "The Edible Wildflower" were born in 1995. The cards depict botanically correct wildflowers with information and recipes on how to use them.

This new line is becoming very popular with kitchen and gourmet food shops, stationery, book and health food stores.

"Here is God's supermarket, blooming in a card rack," says Grette. "I love to see the expression on people's faces when I tell them the flowers are edible. Usually they're delighted and curious and want to know more."

The text on the back of each card tells what parts of the plants to use and how to prepare them. The bookmarks have a full recipe on the reverse.

Grette's botanically correct wildflower renderings have earned several awards in watercolor shows and statewide exhibits.

Until recently, Grette worked in her kitchen or her dining room and faced the frustrating necessity of moving all her supplies and work in progress upstairs to her office, or downstairs to the family room to accommodate the family's frequent guests. When her husband suggested she open an art studio, it didn't take her long to find space.

In November 1994, Grette opened her own studio and art gallery, known as The Old Courthouse Studio and Gallery, in the historical Old Phelps County Courthouse in Rolla, Missouri.

Here she displays her own paintings, and the work of two other artists on a regular basis, along with her notecards, gift enclosures and bookmarks. Each month she features 15-20 works by a popular south central Missouri artist. Her work is also available at the Missouri Botanical Gardens in St. Louis; at Powell Gardens in Kansas City; and at Elm Street Co. in Washington, Mo.

Trudy Jacobson

TRUDY JACOBSON
Tea Berries

Specialty: Antique-style teddy bears sculpted in polymer clay, cast in wood resin, hand-painted, signed and dated by the artist. Larger pieces are numbered. Jewelry, ornaments and figurines.
Medium used: Wood resin.
Price range: $8 to $200

Trudy Jacobson has been a teddy bear artist for 17 years. Her fine arts degree from Bethany College in Kansas provided a background for both the fabric sculpture bears and her current Tea Berries designs.

"Tea Berries" are miniature, old-fashioned bears sculptured in clay and cast in wood resin, which is a mixture of ground pecan shells and resin. Tea Berries are available as jewelry pieces, ornaments and figurines. Pieces range from one to four inches.

"Having made fabric bears since 1979, I needed a design that was bear related, could be reproduced and that would interest bear collectors and gift givers alike. They've been a real hit here and abroad," Trudy said.

The Peter Bear shown is made of polymer clay for the head, paws and boots on a fabric over a wire-armature body. The Tinker Bear he's embracing is also made of polymer clay. This duo won first place at a recent national artists competition.

New designs include the Brushwork Bruins. This bear is made of canvas-quality cotton fabric and painted with oil paints. Treated like an artist's canvas, layers of glazes and individually scrolled hairs create a unique jointed bear with the look of richly carved wood. These are made in limited editions of 25 in six- and ten-inch versions. Trudy also signs and dates each piece, adding to their collectibility. Trudy is also currently working with Sculpey, a polymer clay, and fabric bears with poseable wire armatures.

"I love teddy bears and creating teddy bears. I collect bears and I like to be around other teddy bear artists and bear collectors. Teddy bears are warm and loveable and have as many personalities as the people who collect them," Trudy said.

Trudy has participated in nine European teddy bear shows in Holland, Belgium and Germany while touring with the American Artists for Artists group.

"I enjoy going to Europe to market my creations and find the collectors there as warm and friendly as the American collectors even when we don't speak the same language. A smile and a hug are the same worldwide."

Tea Berries have sold in Europe and have been featured in European and American teddy bear magazines. In 1995, Tea Berries were pictured in *Beer Bericht*, the teddy bear magazine from the Netherlands, and in the U.S. *Teddy Bear Review*. In 1996, her work was featured in *Teddys*, the German teddy bear magazine.

Her work can be seen at teddy bear shows, Cheri's Bear Essentials in Kansas City and Poppy in Columbia.

Shirley Johnson

SHIRLEY JOHNSON
Spoonies, Inc.

Specialty: Historical wooden spoon dolls, paper dolls, a video titled "The Laura Stories."
Media used: Oils and acrylics.
Price range: $100 to $1000

Spoonies, Inc. began in 1988, five years after Shirley lost her cousin, Sara, to cancer. Shirley credits Sara as the real spoon doll maker in the family. In memory of her cousin, Shirley took the spoon doll concept, expanded on it, hired a good lawyer and accountant and went to work.

"I wanted to get even with a life that I felt had dealt a lot of people some nasty blows," she said, "so I began making the dolls to help raise money for cancer research."

She spent hundreds of hours researching the lives of historic American women as well as studying the painting techniques she would use on the spoon dolls. After 18 months of research, Shirley's first line of 68 original Spoonie Dolls was born. This collection now has more than 100 individual spoon personalities.

The unique dolls were an immediate success. Prices range from $100 for the popular Laura Ingalls Wilder doll to $1,000 for such dolls as the Alice Roosevelt Longworth doll, which portrays Alice as a White House

Shirley Johnson

Bride — the lady famous for saying "If you have nothing good to say about anyone, sit right here by me."

Shirley also does special-order museum-quality portrait bride dolls costing from $2,000 to $10,000 each. The proceeds of these dolls are donated to the American Cancer Society.

Each doll has an intriguing history and Shirley is just the person to tell it. With a doll held gently before her, Shirley paints a portrait of life as it was for the historic ladies. Stories range from the popular Laura Ingalls Wilder characters to the tale of Rebecca Boone and her life with pioneer Daniel Boone.

Shirley also takes her story-telling programs on the road with her special fund-raising dollars, taking her dolls each fall in a "Heritage Trunk." She performs for the Doll House at Silver Dollar City, civic groups, clubs, schools and at benefits in her continual fight against cancer.

Shirley's Spoonie Dolls have won several awards, one of the latest being the International Doll Challenge she won with her new Laura Ingalls Wilder paper dolls. Her line of Little Sara Spoonie paper dolls, featuring a child's photo as its face, also won the National Dollmaker's Challenge.

Currently, Shirley is working on Spoonie Doll kits, which will include a painted spoon and instructions as well as a story line about the life of the person portrayed. Also in the works are gift bags, wrapping paper and wearable art such as necklaces and pins.

Her work is available in Missouri at the Laura Ingalls Wilder Museum in Mansfield and at Silver Dollar City in Branson. Her work is also distributed widely throughout the Russian Far East.

Cindy Kuhn

CINDY KUHN
Cindy Kuhn Studio

Specialty: Contemporary folk art, whimsical furniture, painted treatments, custom-fired tile, sinks and dinnerware.
Media used: Wood, latex, acrylic, clay, glaze and found objects.
Price range: $5 to $5,000. Also does commission work.

Cindy's approach to life and art is sparkling and unique.

"I want my art to be smile provoking. I try to use a generous dose of color and humor while creating a useful piece. Even the most utilitarian objects must be artistically interesting, because art should be a part of everyone's life every day," she said.

Cindy's muse surfaces on hand-painted dinnerware, tiles, painted wall and color treatments and custom furnishings. Drawing from a spectrum of over 200 colors and a variety of handmade materials to create her award-winning artwork, Cindy fashions contemporary pieces that are both witty and functional.

The "Nature Chair," for example, sports a rake as one leg, a shovel for the next and has a climbing rose as a centerpiece to her whimsical splashing of color and wit.

Citing such diverse sources as 19th-century poster art, early 20th-century ad-art, the Memphis group and 1930s and 1940s tablecloth motifs

Cindy Kuhn

as the inspirations for her whimsical, graphic style, Cindy describes her work as "deco-functional art."

Cindy Kuhn has been making art furnishings and accessories since she was in the fifth grade. As a former early elementary education specialist and teacher, her playful approach to home decor speaks to the child within us all.

Cindy accepts commissions of all sizes — whether painting a single piece of furniture, working with designers on a special project or creating an entire room.

Margot LeMay

MARGOT LeMAY
Calico

Specialty: Ceramic Old World Santas cast from Missouri clay.
Media used: Ceramics and acrylics.
Price range: $4 to $170

Margot's Old World Santas capture the spirit of Christmas in an array of themes. Margot's series includes Renaissance Santa, Guiding Light Santa, Puppeteer Santa, Buckskin Santa, Victorian Santa and more.

"A love of painting and giving each piece a personality got me interested in this medium. Now, I have a national and international following of collectors," she said.

In addition to Calico's line of 39 Old World Santas, Margot also creates a large variety of Victorian, Southwestern, Native American and seasonal ceramic pieces.

Her shop within the Old Phelps County Courthouse, at 305 West Third Street in downtown Rolla, is the perfect setting to appreciate these art forms of holiday yesteryears.

Margot also acts as a local tour guide and historian.

"We offer tours of the Civil War Era Old Courthouse and the Old Phelps County Jail, both built in 1860 and used by the Union Army. The

Courthouse was used as a hospital and for other military purposes during the Civil War.

"Tours are also offered of the Dillon Log Cabin Museum (circa 1840) which is located across the street. This makes the perfect roadtrip destination to appreciate art and local history all in one afternoon."

Calico Santas are available at Main Street Antiques in Steelville and at the Trading Company of Defiance, in Defiance, Missouri.

Ron Lentz

RON LENTZ
Ron Lentz Fine Woodworking

Specialty: Custom furniture, residential millwork, jewelry, humidors and collectible boxes of hand-selected hardwoods.
Media used: Domestic and imported veneers and lumber.
Price range: $75 to $595 for jewelry boxes. Also does commission work.

    Ron designs and makes collectible jewelry boxes, furniture and an occasional kitchen. He produces work of his own design with a simple, straightforward contemporary style. He also executes work created by other designers on a select basis.
    For 25 years, woodworking was a hobby of Ron's while he practiced architecture. When a friend approached him about some jewelry boxes for a fund-raiser, he said "no problem." Then when he heard the going rate, he said "easy!"

Ron Lentz

As he began to check out the marketplace he was surprised to find very few woodworkers specializing in collectible jewelry boxes.

Five years later, Ron is now selling jewelry boxes coast to coast.

"I had the good fortune in the 80s to have the world's best commercial woodworkers on my architectural projects, like Ray Brochstein in Houston. Only a handful in the country dare call themselves in the same league. Little did I realize then that these were my mentors. Their work was recognizable from a hundred feet away — perfectly matched veneers, clarity and depth of finish."

A trademark of Ron's work is his finishing. Only the clearest finishing products will do. Additives to produce a satin finish only cloud the work, Ron says. A paintbrush is still the tool of choice for all but the largest projects because it allows a speedy buildup of the finish and leaves all of the finishing product on the piece, instead of half in the atmosphere. Since the finish is going to be rubbed out, brush marks are not an issue.

Ron hand selects his woods. He says it's not a chore — it's more like sending a kid to the candy store.

"I buy the best looking lumber available, and inventory it for future needs."

Bill and Jerry Hibdon of Hibdon Hardwoods, a major importer from St. Louis, call Ron when something special turns up. It is this careful selection of materials that makes many of Ron's projects one-of-a-kind, even before the designs are complete.

Sometimes the wood has such a strong character that a design evolves based on the grain alone. The tables pictured in this book are an example.

"The veneer leafs were narrow, with sapwood edges, and a stunning fiddleback grain. The radial pattern created from wedge-shaped cuts seemed like an obvious solution."

Ron emphasizes his ability to create custom furnishing solutions.

"One of my most successful projects was a home for Karen Buckey in St. Louis. After designing her home, I designed and built her kitchen cabinets, dining room furniture, office furniture, fireplace mantles and light fixtures."

Heinrich & Ida Leonhard

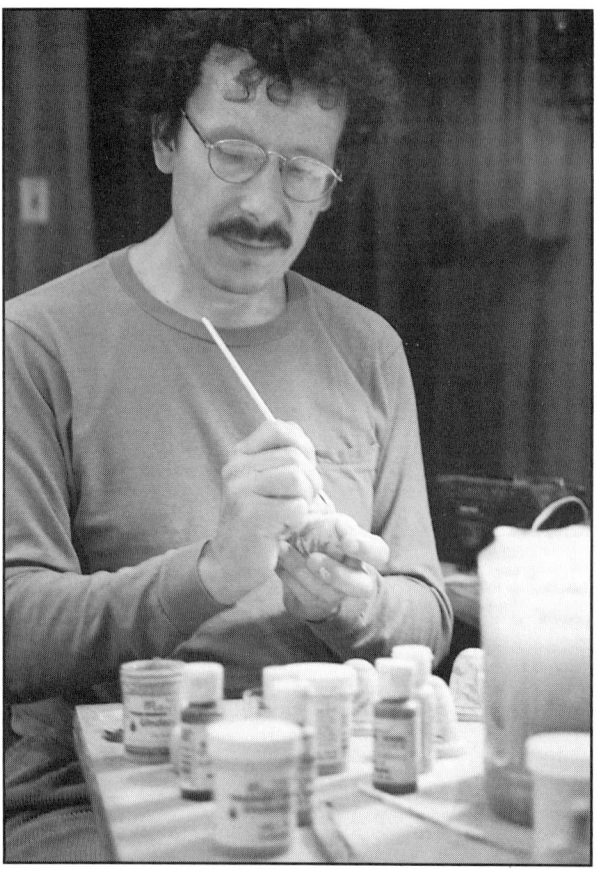

HEINRICH & IDA LEONHARD
Tannenbaum Ceramics

Specialty: Ceramic Christmas ornaments and ceramics for other special occasions.
Media used: Hand-painted ceramics.
Price range: $6 to $100

   Tannenbaum ceramic ornaments are a family tradition. Making ceramic ornaments for the Christmas season and other special occasions has been a way for the Leonhard family to keep in touch with old-time values.
   "Our Old World designs are hand-painted with underglaze colors on earthenware clay cast from original molds. A clear glaze and a durable color-matched ribbon finish each piece. It is our hope that you will enjoy a bit of our German heritage on your own special days," Heinrich said.

Heinrich & Ida Leonhard

"I grew up doing all kinds of handcrafts. My Mom was the big influence there. She made papier-mache puppets and soft sculptured dolls. She even had us knitting for awhile on top of the roof when we were kids. So 17 years ago she took a class in ceramics and started making bells. I came into the business three years after that. I learned how to make molds, starting with her German-influenced designs.

"This tradition has kept us close to our German heritage. We speak German at home, for instance, and we still do some small traditions."

Heinrich says their ornaments appeal to people who respect the time commitment painting each ornament requires.

"People seem to like the fact that there's still somebody doing craftwork basically one at a time. Not mass-producing stuff. The detail work is what sets us apart. We don't seem to have much competition.

"We try to keep coming out with something new. Half the business is bells, and we're starting to appeal to collectors now. In addition to Christmas ornaments, we also make ceramic flutes, trivets, tiles, and ceramic fish.

"We try not to wholesale too much. I like doing fine art and fine craft shows, I think they're great — and a nice way to make a living."

The Leonhards also do area crafts festivals, one in Kentucky and a show in Crested Butte, Colorado.

"I've been to Dallas 500. We do shows with Art Plus in Chicago at the O'Hare Expo Center, the Omaha Summer Arts Festival, and the Renaissance festival in Bonner Springs, Kansas, in the fall."

Their work is available in Columbia at the Columbia Art League, at Bluestem Missouri Crafts, and at Art in the Park in the spring.

Melissa Mallinson

MELISSA MALLINSON
The Feather Merchant

Specialty: One-of-a-kind hair barrettes and brooches made from pheasant feathers and accented with beads and antique buttons.
Media used: Pheasant feathers, antique buttons and beads.
Price range: $8 to $35

The Diamond M Farm, situated in the quiet countryside of north central Missouri is where you'll find the home-based business of Melissa Mallinson. Designing jewelry using pheasant feathers accented with antique buttons and decorative beads lends itself well to the business name The Feather Merchant.

Living on a hunting ranch led to a continual abundance of pheasant feathers.

"The colors in the feathers fascinated me and I looked for a way to display them," Melissa said.

The creation of this jewelry craft came about at a time in 1991 when Melissa was diagnosed with a long-term illness. As a means of focusing on what abilities Melissa was capable of and setting aside the heavy pressure of dealing with her new disability, the creation of pheasant feather jewelry was born.

Melissa Mallinson

"Working in an art form as creative as with the use of feathers can be a challenge," Melissa said. "As each piece of jewelry is designed, it is the color, pattern, curvature and the size of each feather that dictates what is to be created. Feathers are as individualistic as fingerprints and snowflakes, with no two that are alike.

"What amazes me about working with the feathers is that the color of the feather changes like a chameleon on different backgrounds. A blonde feather looks lighter on a blonde than on a brunette. Likewise, when a person puts on one of my brooches, it seems to take on the color of their blouse."

The main emphasis of the jewelry has been barrettes, but customized designs are welcome.

George Manville

GEORGE MANVILLE

Specialty: Replicas of 17th-century watch boxes.
Media used: Walnut, oak, maple, cherry, poplar and pine.
Price range: $85 to $125. Commission work accepted.

    Today, waterproof watches sell for $20. During the 17th century, however, the meticulous, hand-crafted timepieces of the day required diligent care to guard the internal intricacies from the rough world beyond its silver lining.
    Today, George Manville turns back the hand of time re-creating these watch boxes. Made from fine walnut, oak, maple and cherry, these watchcases (or boxes) are patterned after the ones brought to this country and used by the Pennsylvania Dutch in the 17th century.
    Pocket watches at that time had to be held, carried and stored upright

George Manville

to keep them running properly. Watchcases were necessary to secure these rather fragile timepieces at night or to display them during the day in an appropriate place at work or at home. The glass in the door made the watch as well as the time visible to the observer.

Today, they are an excellent way to display an old treasured pocket watch or brooch as well as exhibit a part of our heritage and show craftmanship from the past. The 17th-century craftsman chose different shapes for the openings, and George varies his styles as well, using primarily ovals and heart cut-outs.

Prior to sanding, over 80 different machine and hand cuts are made in the construction of these cases, which are then initialed and numbered.

George taught Industrial Arts for seven years before going to work for the Conservation Department. Upon retirement from the Conservation Department in the near future, the Manvilles will be moving down to the Mansfield, Mo., area. If you are unable to reach them at the listed number, try the local Mansfield operator.

Jim McDonald

JIM McDONALD
JSK Creations in Wood

Specialty: Jewelry boxes.
Media used: Missouri hardwoods and Birds Eye maple.
Price range: $50 and up.

Jim McDonald has been a full-time woodworker since 1980.

"I was working as a timber and log buyer in St. Joseph. Then they had to cut back and laid off three-quarters of their staff," he said.

He turned to his hobby and has never been out of work since.

Jim says exposure in one of the first *Best of Missouri's Hands* catalogs was an early boom to his business. A wood shop in Washington state read the book and ordered several of Jim's jewelry boxes. Now three-quarters of Jim's work is supplying that one store.

He makes jewelry boxes with one, two and three drawers, and some with a tray. Sizes range from large dresser-top boxes to smaller rounded pieces.

He also does several custom jewelry chests on legs each year. His work is finished with hand-rubbed polyurethane, and the interiors are lined with plush velvet. Jim uses burgundy velvet with the darker colored woods and dark green velvet with the cherry and mahogany jewelry boxes.

Jim says that though many people aspire to be full-time woodworkers in their shops, finding the right niche is important.

Jim McDonald

"It's all about hard work and dedication that pull you through, but you've got to find a niche. I've known plenty who work hard and care what they do but they don't find the niche — something to sell to be able to make a living."

Jim has always enjoyed the work, and finds that running his own shop perfectly suits him.

"You have your own schedule. There are seasonal peaks, for instance, this time of year, I'll work from daylight until dark up until Christmas."

He says many types of people enjoy his work.

"I sell to young couples just starting out, older couples who want to give gifts, and to children who have pooled money at Christmas to order for Mom and Dad."

His work is available at Bluestem Missouri Crafts in Columbia, Missouri, and The Wood Merchant, in Laconner, Washington.

Dave & Debbie Milligan

DAVE & DEBBIE MILLIGAN
The County Seat

Specialty: Fine custom woodworking, including staircases, mantels and other high-end custom furniture.
Media used: Hardwoods, including oak, maple, cherry and walnut.
Price range: $500 and up.

Dave and Debbie Milligan realize their artistic expressions one step at a time — literally.

A woodworker for many years, Dave has spent the last seven years building custom staircases.

"Custom staircases are really my specialty. There's no other place in the home that gets such a center stage. You open the front door and 'boom,' there it is," Dave said.

His past commissions are as varied as his clients.

For a doctor's office, he built matching 20-foot desks for the doctor and his secretary. Other times, he builds mantels and accent pieces for the home to match the staircase he constructs.

"Every job is unique, based on the style, location and desires of the home owner," Dave said.

Building the stairs is a trick, Dave says, because "You're using a shop full of high-end furniture saws and planers but you're always on the job doing the work."

"My job is all about the details you don't notice," he said, pointing to the staircase railing. "That feathers imperceptibly to a narrower knob, losing an inch in width in just 18 inches of railing."

Dave completes between 10 and 12 staircases a year in central Missouri. He relies primarily on word-of-mouth advertising.

"The jobs just seem to line themselves up. Right as I finish one, I get another commission," he said. Many times Dave gets less than a week's notice before the construction process actually begins. He has traveled state-wide for his clients. "There are very few people specializing in staircases in the middle of the state."

In addition to operating The County Seat, Dave and Debbie run an antique shop and cafe in downtown Salem.

Toni Moore

TONI MOORE
Artwork Originals

Specialty: Custom portraits of people and pets, Missouri wildlife and western scenes.
Media used: Oil and charcoal pencil.
Price range: $29 to $400

Toni says she paints because "I have art on the brain and can think of nothing else!

"I cannot view the world around me without automatically thinking how I would mix colors to capture the scene on canvas. Just looking up at the sky and seeing the moon starts me wondering how I would paint the soft glow of moonlight as it shines across a stream."

One of her favorite subjects is western art.

"We raise horses and cattle on our rolling Missouri pastures, so as an artist I love to paint western scenes that take place on just another day at work or play."

Toni Moore

She now has available limited edition prints of the western painting entitled "Double Determination." These lithographs show a horse rider trying to rope a wild longhorn in a stubborn war of wills — both determined to win.

"For this painting I wanted the realism and the emotion to jump right off the canvas and charge straight at you! And this western art comes with an attitude. Even someone living in the city can sit back in their chair at the end of a hard-working day and gaze up at the western art on their wall and be drawn into a western state of mind.

"The majority of my work consists of one-of-a-kind-paintings that are created especially for the customer. I specialize in people and pet portraits. Portraits are unique because the finished work has to be exact. I like to paint personality portraits. These portraits tell more about the person, like painting the carpenter swinging his hammer or the little girl playing with her doll or the little boy playing cowboy.

"Pet portraits also have to be exact. For example, to a stranger, three collie pups might look just exactly alike, but the owner would know his pup by its individual characteristics — I love painting these portraits because of the challenge.

"It means a lot to me that people have put their trust in me to create the likeness of their loved ones and I feel the same excitement with every new job that comes along."

Her work can be seen at Artwork Originals Studio in Downing, Lynn's House of Art in Macon, the Gallery On the Square in Lancaster, Mo., and at the Fort Madison Art Gallery in Fort Madison, Iowa.

Shirley Eley Nachtrieb

SHIRLEY ELEY NACHTRIEB
Shirley's Fine Art Studio

Specialty: Watercolor or pastel portraits of individuals, families and homes; portrait dolls also done. Painted by photo or on location.
Media used: Watercolor, pastels or acrylics.
Price range: $175 and up depending on size.

    For the past 25 years, Shirley's primary medium has been watercolor, although "the subject sometimes inspires which medium to use," she said.
    "I aim to create an illusion of inner light in my work."
    She paints mainly from photographs and also does composite work, combining information from more than one photo.
    Her watercolors and pastels portray the subject in loose spontaneity with quiet detail.
    "Each painting develops its own personality as it progresses."
    Her work is in private and corporate collections throughout the United States and Germany.
    She is a member of the Art Section of the St. Louis Artists' Guild, the North Coast Collage Society and the Society of Experimental Artists. She

Shirley Eley Nachtrieb

is also an associate of the Society of Layerists in Multimedia, American Watercolor Society and the National Watercolor Society.

Shirley now lives and works in St. Charles. She began her study of art and education at Michigan State University in 1965. She graduated with honors from Fontbonne College in Clayton, Mo., with a B.A. in education in 1970. After teaching part-time, she began devoting all her time to painting and teaching art workshops.

Shirley is a three-time winner of the prestigious Grumbacher Award. She has studied under well-known master painters Alex Powers, Al Brouillette, Glen Bradshaw, Mary Todd Beam, Tom Lynch and Nita Engles.

She currently teaches art classes and workshops in Missouri and Ohio, and freelances with St. Louis publishers McDonald Publishing and St. Louis Home Builders Association.

In 1996, her work was represented in Rockport Publisher's book *Creative Watercolor* by Mary Ann Beckwith. One watercolor appeared on the cover of the May-June issue of the *Country Register*.

Her artwork has been exhibited at the St. Louis Art Museum, the Chase Park Plaza, Emerson Electric, Ralston Purina, Missouri Athletic Club, Quincy Art Center, Sarasota Visual Arts Center, Reynolds-Heller Gallery in Columbus, the Pump House Art Gallery and numerous juried exhibits.

She is represented by the Augusta Arts Gallery in Augusta, Mo., Barucci Gallery in St. Louis, St. Louis Artists' Guild in Clayton, Mo., St. Peters Cultural Art Center in St. Peters, Mo., and the Pumphouse Art Gallery in Chillicothe, Ohio.

Frank Neef

FRANK NEEF
Pottery by Frank Neef

Specialty: Pottery, crystalline glazed porcelain.
Medium used: Porcelain.
Price range: $8 to $500

South of Springfield outside the town of Highlandville, Frank Neef earns his livelihood making crystalline glazed porcelain.

"I have specialized for the past 14 years in the rare crystalline glaze process. Basically, you are attempting to grow crystals within the matrix of the molten glass glaze.

"These crystals are a zinc silicate structure formed by melting all the glaze materials at approximately 2,400 degrees. I then encourage the crystallization by reducing the temperature to 2,000 degrees."

This temperature is held for five hours to allow the proper conditions for the crystals to grow inside the molten glass. After this, the kiln is shut off and allowed to cool normally. The next day, the pots are unloaded, the base that catches any overflowing glaze is removed and any jagged glass is ground off with a silican carbide grinding wheel.

Frank Neef

"There are less than 50 potters specializing in this rare and beautiful glaze process," Frank said.

He experimented with his glazes until he had "the whitest whites and the bluest blues." But the glaze needs a base. The creation begins, Frank says, when he takes a lump of clay and throws a piece on the wheel.

"Throwing" pots refers to the process of hand-forming a piece on a potter's wheel. This is the step that most people think of as the most involved, but it actually takes only one-fifth of the time that goes into finishing a piece.

A five-year stint as a potter at Silver Dollar City convinced him that he'd found his true love, "next to my wife, Cindy, of course."

Life as an independent potter suits Frank well, but it wasn't easily come by. He tells of spending more than seven years in college. During that time he kept taking classes in pottery "so I could keep my hands in clay.

"I feel real fortunate that somehow I'm able to scratch out a living doing what I like to do."

His work is available at Bluestem Missouri Crafts in Columbia. His work is also at the Smithsonian Museum Shops, in Washington, D.C.

Colleen & Floyd Oglesbay

COLLEEN & FLOYD OGLESBAY
A Serendipity

Specialty: Distinctive hand-painted furniture and accent pieces. Woodworking includes fretwork, furniture, gift items and furniture restoration.
Media used: Oils, acrylics, watercolor, hard and soft woods, exotic woods and weathered wood from old buildings.
Price range: $10 to $2,000. Custom work also accepted.

    Floyd and Colleen are fortunate to have talents and interests that blend together to create unique and beautiful work. Floyd's woodworking takes him in many directions such as delicate fretwork, furniture and gift items.
    "I had access to wood anytime from my father's lumber yard. From my earliest projects I grew to love the feel, the smell, the beauty, the patience and the infinite potential of wood," Floyd said.

Colleen & Floyd Oglesbay

Floyd is a charter member and past president of the Midwest Woodworkers Association.

"When I retired, woodworking became an even more important part of my life. I have run a woodworking shop and I oversee our refinishing shop."

But one of the most enjoyable things he does is to collaborate with Colleen in producing a piece for her to embellish with her quality decorative painting.

"I love a breadth of artistic expression. Watercolors are freeing. I choose the richness of oils for my canvas florals and birds. But what I do most is decorative painting. I use both acrylics and oils depending on the mood and suitability of each piece. I paint on many surfaces, including paper, canvas, porcelain, metal and, of course, furniture," Colleen said.

Colleen is a member of the NSTDP, the National Society for Tole and Decorative Painters, and has studied with several nationally recognized teachers.

"I believe what I do is unique in that I am not aware of other artists who market a high-quality painting on furniture in Mid-Missouri. The painting I do is detailed and executed with artistic care."

Many times, Colleen and Floyd will also choose an old piece of furniture that lends itself to repair and refinishing, which they do in their shop. Colleen then does the finish work of painting it.

Their designs range from authentic European art forms to American primitives, including both realistic and stylized designs. Their retail shop in Missouri River City, Exit 115 on I-70 near Columbia, abounds with examples of each. There you'll also find the work of several other Best of Missouri Hands artists.

Harriet Platz

HARRIET PLATZ
Candles by Hawkins

Specialty: Candle making.
Medium used: Wax.
Price range: $4 to $20

"Corn on the cob, anyone?" Harriet Platz enjoys telling the story of a friend's grandson who started to butter one of her corn candles before he realized it wasn't the eating variety. Her corn candles, modeled after an ear of Indian Corn, are that detailed and realistic.

"I worked with the guy who started this as a hobby and I guess it's kind of gotten out of hand," said Sam Hawkins who owns the business, which is operated by his sister Harriet Platz and her husband, Howard.

It all started as a hobby 20 years ago and has sprouted into a growing business for this Shelbina family. And it's due in large part to the fact that the company has literally kept its "ears" tuned to what customers want.

"Corn is our trademark," Harriet Platz said.

The most popular design is the Corn Candle, which gained popularity with the country look that swept across the nation. They also have more than 65 designs in a variety of colors and scents.

"The business has grown steadily. The year's sales are roughly gauged by the number of tons of wax used. A ton of wax makes 6,000 corn candles and we've gone through quite a few," Harriet said.

Harriet Platz

The wax arrives at the shop in a four-foot cube that the local lumberyard moves with a forklift.

The candle molds are made by Howard, a retired biology teacher, who commented, "This is different than farming, we have a good corn crop every year."

The exquisite detail on the candles is a tribute to the company's practice of pouring and finishing each candle by hand. Harriet says hand pouring is time consuming but makes possible a quality product. The wax is melted in water-jacketed vats and "once you start pouring, you can't stop."

"Our candles are made of a high temperature wax. They burn for hours and won't melt in the trunk."

In addition to the Corn Candle, they have many designs taken from glass, such as toothpick holders, tumblers and crystal vases. One design, the Wizard, is taken from a wood carving and is especially popular with the younger set. Harriet said that one design was even taken from a porch light. "We're always looking for a new unique piece of glass. A lot of them really make nice candles."

Platz and candle maker Rita Homan are constantly experimenting with new colors. Autumn yellow, or roasting ear yellow, is by far their best seller. Every candle is scented and gives off a pleasant aroma whether it is burned or used for decoration. The most popular scent is vanilla.

In Missouri, their work is available at Bluestem Missouri Crafts, Exclusively Missouri in Lee's Summit, Arrowrock Country Store in Arrowrock and The Picket Fence in Crystal City. They have also shipped corn candles to 40 states as well as Canada, England and Japan.

Sam estimated that 90 percent of the candles they sell end up as decorative pieces. "People don't buy candles to burn these days," he said.

Nena Potts

NENA POTTS
"NENA"

Specialty: "Out of the Blue" — Whimsical birdhouse and bird feeder jewelry for the nature lover. Also creates contemporary jewelry designs and Missouri wildflower jewelry in painted leather and other media called "Native Missouri Wildflowers."
Media used: Silver, gold, niobium, brass, copper, gemstones, mixed media and leather.
Price range: $12 and up.

Nena Galloway Potts is a Missouri-born artist and metalsmith who resides in the Ozark woods.

"My surroundings provide an ideal environment for the conception of new and imaginative ideas," she said.

Nena designs tiny whimsical three-dimensional birdhouse earrings and necklaces in a variety of metals and mixed materials. Designs include wren houses of copper and sterling silver, bluebird houses and a window piece, shown above, which is sold as both a pin and necklace.

"These miniature designs are so lifelike that the finch feeder jewelry

Nena Potts

even has real thistle seed inside, tempting any fine feathered friend to take a closer look."

Nena's work encompasses many diverse styles. Her jewelry in gold, silver and niobium has a more serious and contemporary look. Niobium, a key component in much of Nena's work, provides a venue for creating a kaleidoscope of color while experimenting with surface texture and its effects on light reflection.

Combining the high polish or satin finish of gold or silver with the richly colored, heavily textured surfaces of niobium give the work a feeling of depth. The addition of colored stones or found objects to complement the whole provides an endless search for the perfect marriage of color, light, form and function.

Nena received her Bachelor of Fine Arts in 1978 from Southwest Missouri State University. She has been in business since 1981 and has many gallery affiliations throughout the country.

Her work is available at Gypsies in St. Charles, Shepard in the Glen in Glen Allen, Waverly House Gift and Galleries in Springfield, JB Wagner in Kirkwood and at Bluestem Missouri Crafts in Columbia.

Barbara Rasa

BARBARA RASA
The Apple Tree

Specialty: Batik pictures, hand-dyed fabrics and handcast paper ornaments.
Media used: Paper, cloth, wax and dyes.
Price range: $2 to $350

"As our children were growing up, I spent a lot of time in our basement studio working with batik," Barbara said. "They loved to answer my phone calls with 'Yes, Mom's here, but she can't come to the phone right now, she's dyeing in the basement!'

"So-o-o, I'm 'dyeing' to tell you the story of batik. It is an ancient art using dyes and wax-resist to create designs on fabric.

"Because of my daughter's 4-H project which involved driving her 20 miles to a batik class given by New Jersey artist Linda Brick Woytek, who had recently moved to our area, I became deeply interested in the simple but intriguing process of batik."

Barbara remembers going to a Mid Missouri Artists meeting featuring a batik artist. "Batiking totally bored me, but I went anyway. This lady was so full of life . . . She showed us batiking like never before. It was just one of those things that you know you're going to get into."

In the last nine years, batik work and hand-dyed fabrics have become the focal point of The Apple Tree product line.

"Now we make pillows, wearable art, wall hangings, quilts and ornaments. Only our imagination can limit what we can create from the unique batik and hand-dyed fabrics."

With the assistance of two other full-time people, Barbara sends their work to gift shops, florists, antique shops, nurseries, hospitals and to several stores in Japan. She has developed such extensive distribution channels by attending 5 to 6 wholesale gift markets each year.

Their business has done well because there aren't that many batik artists out there, Barbara said. "These fit into the decor of a lot of different homes — mostly Americana, but it's been called folk art too."

Their best-selling batik prints are done with hunter green, burgundy and navy dyes. Earth tones have also been popular colors.

Apple Tree products can be seen at Rustic Yearnings at the Colonnade Shopping Center in Independence and the Touch-A-Heart Shop at the Richmond Hills Shopping Center in Richmond.

Martin Ratermann

MARTIN RATERMANN
Woodworker

Specialty: Heirloom-quality residential, office and church furniture.
Media used: Missouri hardwoods such as walnut, oak and cherry.
Price range: $125 up to $7,500. Commission works vary.

Rocking chairs are fine thrones to slow the pendulum of time. Such a rhythm begins long before the final chair first sways, as Martin blends time-honored principles with meticulous attention to detail.

"I'm not interested in fads or trends. My work is inspired by nature. My forms are found down country roads . . . when there's joy in doing the work, you get paid twice," Martin said.

The joinery, the hand-rubbed finishes, the word-of-mouth marketing and discipline of "no waste," guide his work as much as tools of steel.

"Hand craftmanship is an intimate expression of the spirit of man and provides a link to the human heart. It is time for us to let craft re-emerge as a way in which we as human beings communicate to one another. We have become a spectator society."

This appreciation of process has won Martin acclaim throughout the United States. His commissions grace residences, offices and boardrooms. They are also being found in more and more places of worship.

"I try to help young people become aware of the integrity that should be a part of everyday objects we use and the way we produce them."

Martin Ratermann

Such a sense of heritage is deeply ingrained in Martin, a fourth generation carpenter. He was born and raised in St. Louis where his grandfather built, as well as other St. Louis landmarks, the Tyrolean Alps for the 1904 World's Fair.

Martin has been working in wood for 25 years, first as a finish carpenter, then as a cabinetmaker in a cabinet and architectural woodworking shop. He has had his own shop for 16 years where he has done cabinetry, architectural woodwork and furniture. He continues to learn by attending workshops, sharpening present skills and developing new techniques.

Martin works mostly in American black walnut, the premier wood for fine furniture. He also works in cherry, oak and maple, preferring the rare figured woods when available.

Martin uses a hand-rubbed oil finish that he believes enhances the qualities and safeguards the integrity of these choice hardwoods. It is a mixture of tung oil, linseed oil and satin polyurethane. This finish provides the appeal of an oil finish with the durability of polyurethane. Each piece receives four coats of oil and is then waxed with a mix of tung oil and carnauba wax to reveal all that is beautiful about solid wood: rich color tones, subtle grain patterns and infinite diversity. Each piece is signed and dated.

"The craft of working wood is not just how we make our living, but it is a way of living as well. Satisfaction comes from doing what we think is worth doing, and doing it with integrity. While the work can be physically demanding, it is a true labor of love that provides an alternative to the day-to-day tempo most people experience."

In an era where the machine has provided speed, uniformity, and precision, "creativity has been lost," Martin said. "Hand-crafted pieces are different. They require thought, patience and good taste. These pieces create a relationship between the craftsman, the user, and the material; a relationship that is rare today."

Intimate contact with wood evokes a reverence and sensitivity for the material that transcends the superficial, he said. "We are tools the Creator uses to craft beautiful, functional objects from one of the most precious gifts to the earth, the tree."

Martin's work is characterized by simple lines, rounded edges, sculpted joints and exposed dovetails. "I use very little ornamentation, relying on the figure of the wood grain for that. Simplicity is at the heart of so much that is fine."

His work was featured during the 1996 Missouri River Festival of the Arts in Boonville, Mo.

David & Garlyn Saupe

DAVID & GARLYN SAUPE
Grandview Woolens

Specialty: Wearable woolens — scarves, shawls, throws, hats and booties.
Media used: Wool yarn produced from our flock of Rambouillet sheep.
Price range: $9.50 to $250

Few can dispute the classic look of a natural wool shawl. David and Garlyn Saupe of Grandview Woolens make wool with a twist. Instead of the itchy thing your Grandmother used to wear, the Saupes raise 160 head of Rambouillet ewes, which produce a very soft, "wearable" wool.

Garlyn's trademark is her use of these soft wools in their natural off-white color.

"It's a classic look. It never goes out of style and it goes with everything," Garlyn said. "Plus, there are no irritants from dyes."

The Saupes are following their lifelong dream to farm. They left careers in landscape architecture and teaching to raise sheep, fruit and vegetables and to weave. They drew from former experiences with a small flock of sheep in Washington state to get them started.

The Saupe's flock now produces about 2,000 pounds of high-quality wool each year. The wool is processed into yarn and woven into scarves, throws, shawls and fabric in the time-honored way — on looms by hand.

The unifying thread of past experience that led them to such a profession was curiosity.

David & Garlyn Saupe

"The question in my mind was always 'what's next?' " Garlyn said.

"We always raised the sheep, but I always wondered 'what's next?' when we'd drop the wool off at the warehouse. So I took a class in spinning and learned to make the yarn. And then, of course, I wondered 'what's next?' so I took a weaving class," Garlyn explained.

"It is most satisfying to create beautiful and comfortable products from yarns from our own flock. We've been intimately involved from start to finish. Our loving care for the flock follows through to the finished product," she said.

Now a weaver of 17 years, Garlyn recently received Interweave Press Handweaving Award of Excellence. Her work is on display at Bluestem Missouri Crafts in Columbia, Mo., and at the Missouri Sheep Producers Booth at the State Fair. She also sells from the home by appointment and mail-order.

Another "day at the office" at Grandview Woolens is working the two rambunctious but obedient Border collies with voice commands to round up the sheep and move them from pasture to pasture.

"Those dogs will work those sheep to death if you leave them in there too long," David said. "They live to work those sheep."

The gentle giant of a dog, King, a Great Pyrenees, guards the flock from coyotes and other predators.

And so, what's next for the Saupes? "Developing the selling of these fine articles," Garlyn said. "In addition to working on new ideas and products that are nice to wear, comes the development of the business. What I love is learning every step."

Bonnie Schreckengast

BONNIE SCHRECKENGAST
B & L Baskets

Specialty: Hand-woven baskets, specializing in Cherokee Indian style of weaving.
Media used: Reed, oak, natural materials.
Price range: $10 to $150

Bonnie has been weaving Cherokee-style baskets at her home in Wright City for the past 10 years.

"Most people enjoy the colors and patterns in a Cherokee basket," she said.

The baskets are made mainly of reed, which is a product of bamboo. The basket handles are made from drawn oak. The baskets vary in cost as much as in size. A small, wall basket may be sold for $15 and require an hour of her time to make. Other baskets generally range from $30 to $50.

"I met a family one year that wanted to find a basket that they could tote their dog in," she said. "They tried a variety of baskets until they found the right one. They were so happy to have found the basket . . . and it was just the cutest dog I had ever seen."

Schreckengast gets a lot of requests for her baskets from craft stores but prefers to sell at craft shows. She accepts a few telephone orders.

"I don't like to be committed to producing a certain number of baskets," she explains. "I primarily make the baskets because I love the work, and I really don't want to lose that enjoyment."

"My husband and I love to travel. We'll do six to eight out-of-state shows a year. We also travel extensively looking for baskets," Bonnie said.

Bonnie often turns to her extensive collection of North American Indian baskets for ideas for her next creation.

"I find the history of the baskets interesting, particularly that of the western Indians. It seems when I'm not weaving, I'm planning what I will weave next," she said.

Bonnie also drives a school bus part-time and acts as a foster home for wayward animals that often end up as permanent family members.

Her baskets are available at Bluestem Missouri Crafts in Columbia.

Karen Anne Smith

KAREN ANNE SMITH
When Roses Bloom

Specialty: Hand-painted jewelry, silk, tiles and dinnerware. Portraits on china and porcelain dolls, especially reproductions of antique dolls.
Media used: Porcelain, terra cotta, over and underglaze paints, textiles.
Price range: $5 to $1,500 plus.

Karen Anne makes hand-painted jewelry and silk scarves, hand-decorated dinnerware (earthenware and stoneware platters, pasta bowls, and so on), hand-decorated tiles, wall murals, house numbers and other decorative home and garden accessories. She also paints portraits on china, and on porcelain dolls especially reproductions of antique dolls, and botanically inspired florals using silk and dried materials.

When people ask her how she got started 12 years ago, she replies, "There is something extremely satisfying about the creative process. It goes beyond the money aspect of making a living. I think you can talk to

Karen Anne Smith

any artist and find that they never get paid for the hours involved. So why do we do what we do? It's not for the money. It's not for the public acclaim, because not everyone becomes famous. It's for something deeper, and more satisfying. It's good for the soul. And if the finished work shares a vision of the creative process, we not only serve ourselves but others."

A high spot in her career came when Warner Brothers, in 1993, contacted her for the use of her dolls in the title frames of the movie adaptation of the New York City Ballet's presentation of *The Nutcracker*, starring MacCaulay Caulkin. Other highlights include being nominated for inclusion in the third edition of *American Artists: An Illustrated Survey of Leading Contemporaries*, and in the 1992 edition of *Who's Who Among Rising Young Americans*.

She completed a master's degree in 1992 and is presently working on a doctorate in doll-making through the Doll Artisan Guild, in Oneonto, New York. She is focusing her attention on sculpting and portrait painting on china, presently doing commission works and also designing commercial artworks.

She's a member of the International Doll Artisan Guild, the Global Doll Society, the International Foundation of Doll Makers, the Kansas City Dollmakers Guild and the Daughters of the British Empire.

She has received numerous awards for her work in international professional competitions including the "Millie" and "Gold Rosette," which are the top awards of excellence given by the Doll Artisan Guild. Her commissioned works are in private collections here and abroad, and photographic works have been published in periodicals in the States and overseas. Her work is available at Dalton's Gallery in Overland Park, Kansas, and at Primrose Cottage in California City, California.

Harry Snyder

HARRY SNYDER
Village Pewter

Specialty: Traditional and contemporary lead-free pewter.
Medium used: Pewter.
Price range: $7 to $120

    Harry Snyder makes pewter the same way Paul Revere did, carefully and by hand, using hand-carved molds and a lathe to turn the soft metal into bowls, plates and tankards. "The only real difference today is the electricity we use to turn the lathe."

    In Rocheport, Harry runs Village Pewter in a log building that also houses his wife's quilt frame and quilt notions business. Here are the tools of history — the lathe, melting pot, hard maple wood pieces for carving molds and the sticks to shape the metal as it turns.

    In the four years since his retirement from the University of Mis-

Harry Snyder

souri, he has turned a hobby of 30 years into a business which takes all of his available time.

Each mold, shaped like the inside of a bowl, plate or tankard, takes up to two weeks to carve from hand from hard rock maple. Then it's placed on the lathe and the alloy known as Britannia is worked around the wood form, pressed into shape by applying pressure with wooden sticks while the piece turns at 1,800 revolutions per minute.

The Britannia alloy mix Harry uses has been used safely for dinnerware for more than 300 years. Pewter itself is even older. There are records of pewter vessels in ancient China and Japan over 2,000 years ago. It was a popular metal with the Romans as well. The famous silversmiths Paul Revere, Reed and Barton all started as pewterers. Pewter fell out of fashion at the time of the Revolutionary War with the advent of fine, mass-produced china. Most pewter masters then turned to silversmithing.

"Usually you have to teach people about pewter before they want to buy it," Harry says. When people drop by the Rocheport shop, he will often demonstrate by making a bowl in front of their eyes.

While pewter is considered a soft metal, it is given extra strength by the shape of the bowl or plate. "Traditional designs in pewter often use a rim at the edge of a bowl to give it extra rigidity," Harry said. By hand washing it with dish soap, your pewter plates and bowls can last several lifetimes. Harry also makes baby spoons, Christmas ornaments and jewelry in the shape of thimbles, for stick pins and necklaces.

Because everything is done by hand, it takes a day to turn out six bowls and another day to polish them. With each new design taking two weeks to create, Harry figures he'll be busy for the next few years just getting all the designs he has in his head into the inventory.

In addition to the turned (spun) pieces, Harry also offers hammered pewter trays and bowls in several sizes. The spun pieces include plates ranging from 4" to 12", bowls from 4" to 8" in diameter and a variety of beakers "that's the old-fashioned word for any drinking vessel," says Harry, plus tumblers, stemmed goblets and beer tankards. Pewter is especially good for cold drinks, because once the metal gets cold it stays cold.

If you are planning a trip to Village Pewter, it's best to call first, (573) 698-2102 because Harry and his wife Alice travel quite a bit to quilt shows throughout the country. With advance notice, he is happy to give a demonstration for groups of five or more.

His work was also recently featured in *Rural Missouri,* the publication of the Association of Missouri Electric Cooperatives.

Leandra Spangler

LEANDRA SPANGLER
Bear Creek Paperworks

Specialty: Handmade paper items, including cards, journals, sketchbooks, framed wall art and decorative vessels.
Media used: Handmade paper from recycled and natural fibers.
Price range: $4 to $1,000

Nothing is safe from Leandra's fiber art creations: old blue jeans, odd socks, corn husks, cattails, iris, day lilies, gampi, kozo, flax and yucca all add to the three-dimensional nature of her work.

Whether macerating fibers with a blender or her trolling motor, Leandra uses her special fiber mixes to create one-of-a-kind vessels and cards.

"Once I get my hands wet, I'm hooked," Leandra said.

She works primarily with recycled and natural fibers, but anything is game. "I consider myself a gatherer. I gather ideas, information, people, resources, materials and 'stuff.'"

From her fiber mix, she creates highly textured handmade papers that are then used to cover her one-of-a-kind twine reed vessels.

"I apply a graphite emulsion on top of the textured surface, which I buff to a black sheen.

Leandra Spangler

"I love every step of the papermaking process. I love being wet, preparing the pulps, coloring it, pulling the sheets, pressing and drying them, and finally listening to the rattle of the paper after it's dried. I am excited by the designing challenges of the small space of a note card and the three-dimensional surface of the vessels."

Leandra also makes a line of commercial handmade paper products. Embossed handmade paper cards, multiple monoprint cards, sketchbooks, journals and collages are sold locally and nationwide, with prices beginning at $4. Her journals include an insert with each piece describing the materials used in its construction. Her vessels range in height from 12 to 30 inches and retail for $250 to $1,000.

Her work is available in Columbia at Bluestem Missouri Crafts, Mythmaker Gallery, Legacy Art and Book Works and at the Columbia Art League. In Springfield, her work is available at the Walnut Street Gallery.

Dawn Steuck

DAWN STEUCK
Prairie Country

Specialty: Authentic period, highly detailed corn husk dolls.
Media used: Corn husks, corn silk and accessories.
Price range: $12.50 to $50

For 11 years, Dawn has shucked more traditional craft pursuits in order to produce highly detailed corn husk dolls in period costume.

"Exquisite detailing is the most fun in creating each doll — no two are exactly the same," Dawn said.

Corn husk dolls were originally made and used by the American Indians. These primitive dolls were crafted without faces due to superstitions. Now, 200 years later, interest in corn husk dolls has rekindled, and it has become fashionable to collect them.

Dawn keeps busy with the growing interest. Prairie Country Corn Husk Dolls now offers a wide selection of country, Victorian and specialty dolls. They come in natural tints, as well as an array of colors or color combinations, and Dawn says personal requests are most welcome. Each doll is also named and numbered.

Prairie Country corn husk dolls rekindle thoughts of past traditions and simplicity for present-day doll lovers and collectors.

Dawn Steuck

"From start to finish, they're a perfect doll, a perfect gift, a perfect memory created," Dawn said.

Dawn started making corn husk dolls 11 years ago.

"My sister sent a very simple, plain corn husk doll to me for my birthday. I thought I could probably make one, since I've always liked to do arts and crafts . . . anything creative," Dawn said. "We are a farming family and grow corn so I had an unlimited amount of corn husks to fool around with.

"My first dolls were very primitive. However, one day my church had a ladies' salad supper and asked me to decorate the tables with fall decor. I made several dolls and they were a hit!"

Through the years, Dawn's dolls have changed.

"I have developed a style that is easily recognizable. My dolls are highly detailed and elaborate. I've sold coast to coast and even sent some to Norway. Collectors are becoming more interested in my dolls.

"Since these dolls are quaint, one-of-a-kind pieces, I don't mass produce them. Each doll takes several hours to create," Dawn said. "With that in mind, along with substitute teaching full-time and being a farmwife and Mom, I can't produce zillions of dolls. I'm a very tiny business. My shop is in my home. A phone call before visits is preferred, though drop-ins are welcome."

Elaine Taylor

ELAINE TAYLOR
Folk Art

Specialty: Wood carvings, sculpting and illustrations.
Media used: Wood, basswood, sugar pine, papier-mache, pen & ink.
Price range: $10 to $650

"The first thing I ever carved was a piece of my mother's homemade lye soap," Elaine said. "Somehow I don't think my Mom was so impressed with the outcome of her logo — a witch on a broom flying across the moon. It was nothing personal, Mom!"

It wasn't until her late twenties, working for the Missouri Botanical Gardens, that she began carving on a larger scale.

"It was here I suppose I carved my first real carving. I used an 8' by 2' by 6" slab of styrofoam and carved it into an 8' nutcracker for a Christmas show I had organized. It was wrapped in plaster to look like wood, then painted. I also carved out a large rocking horse and toy drum to stand with the nutcracker.

"People really loved the props and to my surprise a lot of publicity came from that show. The Nutcracker appeared in magazines, newspapers, posters and even on Christmas cards sold at MBG's gift show. He became quite popular, and they still use him, some thirteen years later.

"That was in 1983 and never again did I carve until August 1994. I mostly did illustrations for educational exhibits. When I gave up my career

Elaine Taylor

in horticulture in 1984 it was in the interest of going on to bigger and better things — a family. In 1986, our son Jacob was born. Fifteen months later, our daughter Monica was born.

"I had plenty of time to make a career for myself before they came. The plan was for me to be a full time Mom. I really value that idea because my Mom was always there for us when we grew up. But financially it didn't cut it. I started to find things I could do at home. I dabbled in sculpting things in acrylic clay.

"My dear friend and mentor, Carole Behrer, kept prodding me to send some of my work to a gallery in Chicago where she sent her work. The women who owned the shop was very interested to my surprise, but she kept insisting I do these sculptures in wood.

"My husband came home from work one day with a block of wood and an Exacto knife. The first woodcarving was a very primitive cat. Then I couldn't carve enough of them. Now they are still selling well during "cat month" in Chicago as the "Whittington Cats."

"Many cuts and 911 calls later, I've found much better tools. I'm having a lot of fun as long as I don't bleed. The most gratifying part is when someone picks up a piece of my work, looks it over and has to have it because they love it.

Her carvings include both animal and nature themes.

"When I carve, there is usually always some kind of animal involved in the carving. I think that's what appeals to the majority of people who buy my work. They see animals they love too."

Her work is available at Bluestem Missouri Crafts in Columbia and at Hog Hollow in Chesterfield.

Julia Taylor & Don Sumpter

JULIA TAYLOR & DON SUMPTER
Woodworks FolkArt

Specialty: Folk art ornaments, decorative spindles, candlesticks which celebrate the seasons. Limited edition fiber works in wool, silk and cotton (clothing and bags) & other small works.
Media used: Wood, acrylic paints, pens, wool, silk & cotton.
Price range: Ornaments from $10. Candlesticks from $20. Fiberworks by special order only.

Julia has been making ornaments for over ten years. Using orphaned wood pieces, she and Don create things which have a second chance as artwork. The ornaments grew out of the original *Kinderkuchen* ornaments which were made from clay dough, featured at the Bird in Hand and Neiman Marcus stores in St. Louis.

"I've always loved folk art and the color families used in these gentle

Julia Taylor & Don Sumpter

forms. The ornaments and candlesticks are my interpretation of Christmas folk birds, angels, moons, stars and nearly 300 designs that have been done over the last 10 years. Our customers add ideas about things they want and we also take inspiration from the countryside where we live in the woods," Julia said.

"I've always been an artist and now I am able to devote most of my time to this work. All the things I have learned and seen and experienced have added to the things I make. My artwork is like mental geology, layers of ideas and events and thoughts embodied in the things I paint."

"The woodworking is all Don's. All the painting is mine. It's very personal. We are tiny . . . just two people, cutting, sanding, painting, selling. It's demanding and rewarding — a lifelong dream to do the work I love the best and be what I am. It's very hard to talk about myself. It's very easy to paint what I think and feel. I am my art, its an extension of me.

"The wood and paints open up endless possibilities of design. The candlesticks and spindles offer the chance to work in 3-dimensional shapes. We are always searching around for old wood turnings and pieces which look right for our work.

"Christmas is our busiest time, but we now make baby things, spring and summer pieces and garden pieces. I find the complimentary fiber pieces are a pleasant diversion. The move to the country five years ago has been wonderful. Our lives out here revolve around the seasons and so does the artwork.

"Our newest designs are a set of small birds which are painted from the ones we see at the feeders by our windows and those who live here in the summer and winter. The garden candlesticks are after our own gardens. . . the vegetables, herbs and flowers which we grow.

"We have been very fortunate to have our own work in shops, stores and galleries and museum shops across the country. We do shows, too, which give us the chance to meet so many people. We have been featured in several magazines, including *Better Homes and Gardens*, *Country Crafts*, *Decorative Woodcrafts* and *Decorative Painter*.

"*Best of Missouri Hands* has been a network of friends and resources which helped us go forward and keep our spirits up when the spirit of an artist needs a bit of uplifting."

Woodworks FolkArt is available at Neiman Marcus in St. Louis, Bluestem Missouri Crafts in Columbia, It's a Small World in Kimmswick, Down by the Station in Kirkwood and the Cathedral Shop in St. Louis. Work is also at the St. Louis Art Museum Gift Shop during the Christmas season.

Kathleen & Michael Weltzin

KATHLEEN & MICHAEL WELTZIN
Willow Works

Specialty: Traditional and fanciful one-of-a-kind twig gifts, creations and furniture of bent willow, white birch and twisted sassafras for home, garden and lodge.
Media used: Branches, tree trunks, birch skin and vines.
Price range: $8 and up.

  Willow Works' fanciful twig furniture and folk art creations blend with any decorating style, indoors or out. Like people, no two trees are exactly alike, making each item truly unique.
  "At Willow Works we handcraft a variety of bent-willow, white birch and twisted sassafras creations for home, garden and lodge," Kathleen said. "I spot any branch or trunk with a crazy twist from a mile away. When you

go on nature trails and you see a woman with big hair running wildly through the woods with loppers open — that's me gathering my forest treats."

Bent willow furniture was a common sight on porches until the 1930s. Gypsy travelers pulled their wagons from town to town, often building and peddling their wares, hence the nickname "gypsy twig furniture."

The "Once Upon a Time Chair," at left, with Fairie Gazebo and chair basket was created as a tribute to fairies, gnomes and trolls, Kathleen says.

"At the Missouri Botanical Garden Expo, a robin gathered moss and twigs from vendors' booths and built a nest in the gazebo!"

The "Twisted Bed" below is made of twisted sassafras trunks and hop vine. The glass-top bed tray is made of willow.

"We build while the wood is still green. Because of willow's pliable nature, the furniture designs are virtually unlimited, allowing for great comfort and style. Sassafras trees have been choked by vines embedded into the bark. This forms a deeply etched, twisted spindle up and down the trunk — Nature's magic!

"We haul our fallen white birch from Beaver Island in Lake Michigan where I spent my childhood. Surrounded by old log cabins, forest and legends, it's where my passion for rustic furniture began.

"Try a trellis on an inside wall or one of our beds on a screened in porch. Our designs blend with any style."

Kathleen also hosts two art festivals each year in the spring and autumn. Her work has been featured in *Better Homes and Gardens*, *Country Garden*, Europe's *Amica* and *St. Louis* magazine.

Work is available at their "open-air" studio and is built on site.

Jenna Weston

JENNA WESTON
Gathering Root Basketry

Specialty: Unique and contemporary baskets and sculptural vessels.
Media used: Handmade paper, Missouri roots and vines.
Price range: $45 to $500

Transforming the commonplace and finding the mythic within the mundane is Jenna's pursuit with basketry.

"In order to do this, I need to transform some of this earthy, ordinary stuff into new patterns that have been given new stories to tell. I use mundane materials like sticks and vines in a manner that will make people pay attention to them in a new way. I rearrange their original patterns, making unusual combinations of different elements and add other non-indigenous media. The ordinary is thus transformed into the extraordinary."

"I come from the woods, hills and fields, arms laden with their trea-

Jenna Weston

sures. I see it as my task in this life to remind people of our connection to the earth. In this age of synthetics, mass-production throw-aways and 'virtual realities,' I feel a need to reassert the value of that which is lasting, unique and real," she said.

In the late 60s, Jenna earned her BFA degree from Michigan State University. This provided her with a strong foundation from which to experiment and innovate her work.

"My basket making background is rooted in tradition. I learned from various teachers the basic techniques and styles of traditional Appalachian and Ozark baskets: twined, plaited, ribbed and flat-split basket weaving. I honed my skills and refined my craftmanship within these traditional parameters.

"As I pushed the boundaries of the physical form beyond utilitarian, the basket has evolved into a 'vessel' — a container for spirit rather than for objects. I am interested in revealing what holds things together, what goes on behind the scenes."

Jenna also makes all her own paper and gathers and prepares all the vines and roots from the land around her farm in the Ozarks, often while on horseback. She also grows some of the plants she uses to make paper on her farm.

Her work is available at Bluestem Missouri Crafts in Columbia.

Annie Young

ANNIE YOUNG
Hidden Peace Farm

Specialty: Handmade, hand-dyed baskets in a variety of styles and sizes.
Media used: Rattan reed, oak hoops, native vines and plants of all types.
Price range: $15 to $500. Will do commissions.

Nestled in the rolling hills of the upper Ozarks lies Hidden Peace Farm. Glenn and Annie Young own and operate this working farm where they care for cattle, hogs, poultry and waterfowl in a tranquil setting. Over the past six years it's also come to be known for the beautiful, colorful and functional baskets that are made there.

Tradition is important at the farm. A self-taught artist, Annie is a full-time basketmaker, and does all her dyeing and weaving by hand. She offers traditional and contemporary designs in a full range of colors. She also offers home consulting where she will design and create baskets to suit a customer's personal decor. Annie hand-dyes her reed in personally mixed colors and can, therefore, blend colors to suit the special needs of her customers.

Annie, who has worked in various mediums through the years, says her husband is responsible for her becoming a basket weaver.

"He likes to teach himself various skills which he usually abandons once he's mastered them. He bought a small how-to pamphlet on weaving

Annie Young

an egg basket and taught himself. Then he taught me. Once he'd made several baskets, he was done, but I was hooked.

"I began making baskets and gave them to relatives as gifts. They would show them to their friends and soon strangers were calling me and asking me to make something for them. Before I knew it I was dragged into business and having to learn a whole new set of skills as a business professional . . . I'm still working on this one.

"The varied designs and the endless variety of color combinations keep me constantly excited. I'm always trying something new. I'm now working on some of my own designs, experimenting with natural dyes and native weaving materials and delving into basket history. I work hard at keeping what people want and yet moving forward with fresh and interesting materials," she said. Her pursuit of fresh ideas won her an Award of Excellence at the recent St. Louis Art Happening art exhibit.

In the fall, Annie ventures into the woods to collect wild grapevines to be used as handles in her egg baskets. In winter, you'll find a pot of stew simmering on the wood cookstove, bread rising on the counter, and Annie, the basket enthusiast, delving into old texts in search of basket lore and historic designs to be used in creating new and exciting forms. She is currently working on original contemporary designs in addition to her popular traditional designs, all in a vivid variety of colors.

Life moves at a different pace in this secluded oasis, and those who venture into their world know why the Youngs have come to call it home.

"Everyone is made welcome, and they leave with more than a beautiful, handmade basket," Annie said. "They also receive a deep sense of well-being, a glimpse into a way of life that has long been forgotten, and the knowledge that no other name could more aptly describe this place called Hidden Peace Farm."

Supporting members throughout Missouri

Juried Member Addresses

1. BARKSDALE, JAMES
Heritage Collection
P.O. Box 35
Steelville, MO 65565
(573) 775-2027
Studio is inside Willie Mole's Antique Shop, 105 East Main, downtown Steelville. Open to public 10-5 daily. Closed on Monday.

2. BARNES, MARILYN
Adornments by Marilyn
3512 South Fort
Springfield, MO 65807
(417) 887-1608
Studio not open to the public.

3. BEHRER, CAROLE
Traditional Crafts
2315 Gray Summit Rd.
Pacific, MO 63069
(314) 742-2369
Studio not open to the public.

4. BENJAMIN, MARY
Designs in Clay
1108 South Glenwood
Columbia, MO 65203
(573) 449-1630
Studio open to public by appointment only.

5. BLAND, STEVE
Aseity Kaleidoscopes
1531 Washington Ave. #9 G
St. Louis, MO 63103
(314) 436-4242
Studio open to public by appointment only.

Juried Member Addresses

6. BOSCHERT, SERENA
Serena Boschert
714 Washington St.
St. Charles, MO 63301
(314) 946-1874, call anytime
Home studio, not open to the public.

7. BRACK-KAISER, CAROL LEIGH
Carol Leigh's Specialties and Hillcreek Fiber Studio
7001 Hillcreek Rd.
Columbia, MO 65203
(573) 874-2233
Open to public. Monday through Friday 9 a.m. to 5 p.m.
Located: Two miles south of Columbia, Mo. Take Providence Road South (exit off I-70) all the way through Columbia. Providence Road becomes Route K. Stay on K for 1 1/4 miles. Turn left on Hillcreek Road. We are one-half mile down Hillcreek on the right — the only house in the bottoms before Little Bonne Femme Creek.

8. BRAUN, RICK & SUE
Wood Merchant
Hoot Owl Point
HCR 3, Box 388
Kimberling City, MO 65686
(417) 739-2420 or (417) 779-5324
toll free 1-888-WOOD-MER (966-3637). Fax (417) 739-2420.
Shop location: Jct 86W & 13S, Lampe, Mo. By appointment only.

9. CANHAM, VICKIE
Aesthetic Arts Studio
4445 Roemer Rd.
Columbia, MO 65202
(573) 442-8033
Studio open to public by appointment only.

10. CLEMENS, BRUCE & CATHY
Silver Feather Jewelry
P.O. Box 165
Galena, MO 65656
(417) 357-6528. Fax (417) 357-6528. E-mail: bclemens@mail.orion.org
Studio open to public by appointment only.

Juried Member Addresses

11. COPLEY, CONNIE
The Con Artist
854 Newport
Webster Groves, MO 63119
(314) 961-7192
Studio not open to the public.

12. CRUME, ANN
Paper Chase
Box 16555
Kansas City, MO 65133
(816) 455-8753
Studio not open to the public.

13. DENMAN, DIANA
Wolf's Point Studio
Rt. 1, Box 3770
Lupus, MO 65046
(816) 849-2582
Open to public. Monday through Friday, 10 a.m. to 4 p.m., call first. Location: From Columbia, take I-70 west to Exit 179, turn south and drive approximately 11 miles to Route P, turn left, follow blacktop 4 miles into Lupus. Studio is the second building on the left on Main Street. From Jefferson City, get on Highway 50, take 179 north until you reach Route P and follow it 4 miles into Lupus.

14. EISENHAUER, DODIE
Village Designs
310 State Hwy AA
Daisy, MO 63743
(573) 266-3642. Fax (573) 266- 0412
Studio open to public by appointment only.

15. ERNST, JEWEL & WILLIAM
Loutre Valley Enterprises
P.O. Box 113
Montgomery City, MO 63361
(573) 564-2493
Open to public.

Juried Member Addresses

16. FEAGINS, PEGGY
OakLeaf Pottery
13213 Bennington Ave.
Grandview, MO 64030
(816) 761-7419
Studio open to public by appointment only.

17. FERBER, LEE & PAM
Peola Valley Pottery
Rt 1, Box 16-F
Lesterville, MO 63654
(573) 637-2507
Open to public.

18. FISCHER, JEANNETTE
Designs by Jeannette
P.O. Box 14
Lohman, MO 65053
(573) 782-4594
Studio not open to the public.

19. FRAZIER, MARY
Ancient Images
Route 4, Box 64A
Eldon, MO 65026
(573) 392-7189
Studio open to public by appointment only.

20. GIBSON, MEG
Gibson Glass Bead
1500 Richardson St.
Columbia, MO 65201
(573) 443-3352
Studio not open to the public.

21. GORMAN, STEVE
Painted Sculptures
212 W. Halliburton
Independence, MO 64050
(816) 461-7097
Studio open to public by appointment only.

Juried Member Addresses

22. HERRICK, GRETTE
Old Courthouse Studio and Gallery
708 Salem Avenue
Rolla, MO 65401
Studio: (573) 364-0814. Office: (573) 364-3212. Fax (573) 368-2817
e-mail: grette@rollanet.org http:/www.rollanet.org/~grette
Open to public.

23. JACOBSON, TRUDY
Tea Berries
7801 Wade School Road
Columbia, MO 65202-9665
(573) 442-5044
Not open to public.

24. JOHNSON, SHIRLEY
Spoonies, Inc.
2203 Thomas Rd.
Norwood, MO 65717
(417) 746-4800
Studio open to public by appointment only.

25. KUHN, CINDY
Cindy Kuhn Studio
12794 W. Watson
Sunset Hills, MO 63127
(314) 843- 4932
Studio open to public by appointment only.

26. LeMAY, MARGOT
Calico
Court Square
305 W. 3rd Street
Rolla, MO 65401
(573) 364-2187
Store is open to the public, Tuesday through Saturday, 11 a.m. to 3 p.m. or by appointment. Closed January and February.
Directions: Entering Rolla from I-44, take Hwy 63 South to Hwy 72. Turn left on Hwy 72. Go approximately 4 blocks to four-way stop. Turn left on Rolla Street. Go three blocks then turn left on Third Street.

Juried Member Addresses

27. LENTZ, RON
Ron Lentz Fine Woodworking
2122 Victor Street
St. Louis, MO 63104
(314) 664-5940 or (314) 664-3531
Open to public.

28. LEONHARD, HEINRICH & IDA
Tannenbaum Ceramics
218 E. Parkway
Columbia, MO 65203
(573) 449-1043
Studio open to public by appointment only.

29. MALLINSON, MELISSA
The Feather Merchant
Diamond M Farm
Rt. 1, Box 242
Princeton, MO 64673-9801
(816) 748-3558
Studio not open to the public.

30. MANVILLE, GEORGE
Rt. 5, Box 242A
Mexico, MO 65265
(573) 581-6755
Studio not open to the public.

31. McDONALD, JIM
JSK Creations in Wood
4901 Highway D
Farmington, MO 63640
(573) 756-3239
Studio open to public by appointment only.

32. MILLIGAN, DAVE & DEBBIE
The County Seat
201 E. Fourth St.
Salem, MO 65560
(573) 729-8325
Studio open to the public by appointment only. Studio is at the corner of Fourth and Iron Streets in downtown Salem near the old courthouse.

Juried Member Addresses

33. MOORE, TONI
Artwork Originals
RR 2, Box 112
Downing, MO 63536-9535
(816) 379-2787 or (816) 379-2690
Studio open to public by appointment only on Highway 136 in Downing.

34. NACHTRIEB, SHIRLEY ELEY
Shirley's Fine Art Studio
908 Ruth Drive
St. Charles, MO 63301
(314) 947-1936
Studio open to public by appointment only.

35. NEEF, FRANK
Pottery by Frank Neef
1719 Hawthorne Rd.
Highlandville, MO 65669
(417) 443-3861
Studio open to public by appointment only.

36. OGLESBAY, COLLEEN & FLOYD
A Serendipity
4070 N. Roemer Rd.
Columbia, MO 65202
(573) 449-8336 or (573) 874-0901
Their shop at Missouri River City is now open to the public.
Location: Rocheport Exit 115 on I-70, near Columbia.

37. PLATZ, HARRIET
Candles by Hawkins
101 E. Walnut, P.O. Box 346
Shelbina, MO 63468
(573) 588-4008 or 4731
Studio open to public weekdays 9:30-4:00, Saturdays 9:30-noon.

38. POTTS, NENA
"NENA"
4205 E. Farm Rd. 172
Rogersville, MO 65742
(417) 886-7757. Fax (417) 886-9423
Studio open to public by appointment only.

Juried Member Addresses

39. RASA, BARBARA
The Apple Tree
Rt. 1, Box 122A
Higginsville, MO 64037
(816) 584-7379
Studio open to public by appointment only.

40. RATERMANN, MARTIN
Woodworker
300 McRoberts Street
Boonville, MO 65233
(816) 882-2695
Studio open to public by appointment only.

41. SAUPE, DAVID & GARLYN
Grandview Woolens
34560 Mabry Rd.
Bucklin, MO 64631
(816) 695-3290
Studio open to public by appointment only.

42. SCHRECKENGAST, BONNIE
B & L Baskets
888 Schreckengast Rd.
Wright City, MO 63390
(314) 745-3226
Studio open to public by appointment only.

43. SMITH, KAREN ANNE
When Roses Bloom
4501 South Sterling Ave.
Kansas City, MO 64133
or P.O. Box 22614, Kansas City, MO 64113
(816) 358-1410. Pager (816) 247-9504
Studio open to public by appointment only.

44. SNYDER, HARRY R.
Village Pewter
210 N. Central St.
Rocheport, MO 65279-0150
(573) 698-2102
Studio open, Monday to Saturday 9-5, Sundays 1-5.

Juried Member Addresses

45. SPANGLER, LEANDRA
Bear Creek Paperworks
405 W. Texas
Columbia, MO 65202
(573) 442-3360
Studio open to public by appointment only.

46. STEUCK, DAWN
Prairie Country
Rt. 3, Box 117
Rich Hill, MO 64779
(417) 395-4267
Studio open to public by appointment only.
Directions: Go west through Rich Hill, turn south on blacktop PP 1-3/4 miles. They are the second house on road (a two-story white farmhouse).

47. TAYLOR, ELAINE
Folk Art
660 Riverview Rd.
Labadie, MO 63055
(314) 742-4325
Studio not open to the public.

48. TAYLOR, JULIA, & DON SUMPTER
Woodworks FolkArt
HC88, Box 8536
Steelville, MO 65565
Phone and fax (573) 743-6627
Studio not open to the public.

49. WELTZIN, KATHLEEN & MICHAEL
Willow Works
830 Marshall Avenue
Webster Groves, MO 63119
(314) 963-9417
Studio open to public by appointment only.

Juried Member Addresses

50. WESTON, JENNA
Gathering Root Basketry
Rt. 5, Box 934
Ava, MO 65608
(417) 683-3610
Studio open to public by appointment only.

51. YOUNG, ANNIE
Hidden Peace Farm
Rt. 1, Box 220
Meta, MO 65058
(573) 793-6613
Studio open to public by appointment only.

Full Membership List

BARKSDALE, JAMES. Heritage Collection, P.O. Box 35, Steelville, MO 65565. (573) 775-2027. Hand-carved birds made of Missouri woods.

BARNES, MARILYN. Adornments by Marilyn, 3512 South Fort, Springfield, MO 65807. (417) 887-1608. Handcrafted jewelry from antique and vintage buttons.

BATTON, SUE. Dove Creations, P.O. Box 32, Wooldridge, MO 65287. Flame-colored copper artwork.

BEHRER, CAROLE. Traditional Crafts, 2315 Gray Summit Rd., Pacific, MO 63069. (314) 742-2369. Theorem painting and *scherenschnitte* in grain-painted frames.

BENJAMIN, MARY. Designs in Clay, 1108 South Glenwood, Columbia, MO 65203. (573) 449-1630. Contemporary porcelain jewelry using millefiore technique.

BLAND, STEVE. Aseity, 1531 Washington Ave. #9 G, St. Louis, MO 63103. (314) 436-4242. Wildflower kaleidoscopes.

BLISS, BARBARA & CLIFFORD. American Stone Art, Route 1, Box 209B, Louisiana, MO 63353. (314) 754-3272. Hand-modeled and sculpted stone animals.

BOSCHERT, SERENA. Serena, 714 Washington St., St. Charles, MO 63301. (314) 946-1874. Custom Christmas ornaments with portraits of house and pet.

BRACK-KAISER, CAROL LEIGH. Carol Leigh's Specialties and Hillcreek Fiber Studio, 7001 Hillcreek Rd., Columbia, MO 65203. (573) 874-2233. Custom weaving, spinning and natural dyeing.

BRAUN, RICK & SUE. Wood Merchant, Hoot Owl Point, HCR 3, Box 388, Kimberling City, MO 65686. Shop: Jct 86W & 13S, Lampe, MO. (417) 739-2420 or (417) 779-5324. Toll free 1-888-WOOD-MER (1-888-966-3637). Fax (417) 739-2420. Fine quality driftwood furnishings.

Full Membership List

BRICHETTO, CYNTHIA. 8009 Appleton, Raytown, MO 64138-2242. (816) 358-9429. Hand-sculpted Old World Santas, sculpture jewelry and miniatures.

BRIDGER, RUTH ANN. Ruth Ann's Bears, 6943 Waterman, St. Louis, MO 63130. (314) 727-6451. Collector Teddy Bears of mohair and other fabrics.

CANHAM, VICKIE. Aesthetic Arts Studio, 4445 Roemer Rd., Columbia, MO 65202. (573) 442-8033. Fine porcelain giftware, portraits and custom ceramic tile.

CLEMENS, BRUCE & CATHY. Silver Feather Jewelry, P.O. Box 165, Galena, MO 65656. (417) 357-6528. Fax (417) 357-6528.

COPLEY, CONNIE. The Con Artist, 854 Newport, Webster Groves, MO 63119. (314) 961-7192. Unique one-of-a-kind jewelry designed from vintage and contemporary findings.

COWELL, LINDA. The Oak Creek Company, 1177 Colby Court, St. Peters, MO 63376. (314) 447-2718. Original design St. Nicholas figurines & angels from vintage linens, quilts and trims.

CRUME, ANN. Paper Chase, P.O. Box 16555, Kansas City, MO 65133. (816) 455-8753. Handmade and recycled paper, papermaking equipment and products.

DENMAN, DIANA. Wolf's Point Studio, Rt. 1, Box 3770, Lupus, MO 65046. (816) 849-2582. Wheel-thrown and slab-built functional and decorative stoneware.

EISENHAUER, DODIE. Village Designs, 310 State Hwy AA, Daisy, MO 63743. (573) 266-3642. Fax (573) 266-0412. Wire-mesh angels, bows and ornaments.

ERNST, JEWEL & WILLIAM. Loutre Valley Enterprises, P.O. Box 113, Montgomery City, MO 63361. (573) 564-2493. Basketry, caning, woodworking and framing.

EVERETT, CHARLOTTE. Tightwad Pottery, 346 SE Hwy PP, Clinton, MO 64735. (816) 477-3793. Hand-built and wheel-thrown pottery.

Full Membership List

EWERTZ, JANET. The Light House, 1301 Walnut, Higginsville, MO 64037. (816) 584-6416. Unique handcrafted quality table lamps.

FAUST, LESLIE. Faust Graphics, 5 Plant Ave. Suite #2, St. Louis, MO 63119. (314) 647-2228. Pen and ink, watercolor drawings.

FEAGINS, PEGGY. OakLeaf Pottery, 13213 Bennington Ave., Grandview, MO 64030. (816) 761-7419. Functional, hand-thrown stoneware pottery.

FERBER, LEE & PAM. Peola Valley Pottery, Rt 1, Box 16-F, Lesterville, MO 63654. (573) 637-2507. Handmade stoneware pottery, earthenware Christmas ornaments and ceramic jewelry.

FISCHER, JEANNETTE. Designs by Jeannette, P.O. Box 14, Lohman, MO 65053. (573) 782-4594. Applique sweatshirts.

FRAZIER, MARY. Ancient Images, Route 4, Box 64A, Eldon, MO 65026. (573) 392-7189. Gourds rendered and aged in various media.

GIBSON, MEG. Gibson Glass Bead, 1500 Richardson St., Columbia, MO 65201. (573) 443-3352. Lampworked glass, specializing in one-of-a-kind beads.

GOGGINS, ROBERT. Beauty in Leather, Rt. 1, Box 400, Ellington, MO 63638. (573) 924-2469. Hand-carved and stained leather art.

GORMAN, STEVE. Painted Sculptures, 212 W. Halliburton, Independence, MO 64050. (816) 461-7097. Sculptor.

GRANT, ANITA. Windy Hill Studio, 4244 S. 205th Rd, Halfway, MO 65663. (417) 445-2606. Fiber-weaving, silk-painting and felting.

GREER, ARLENE. The Silk Shop, Rt. 1, Box 1010, Shell Knob, MO 65747. (417) 858-6399. Silk and dried flowers arranged in exotic baskets.

HARDIN, KATHLYN. Bear Tales, 13517 S. Phelps, Independence, MO 64055. (816) 373-2293. Handmade teddy bears with fur, joints and personality.

HAUSMAN, GREGORY. Star-Joy, HCR 62, Box 49B, Hermann, MO 65041. (314) 943-2227 or (314) 943-6466. Whimsical Santas created in chalkware and hand-painted or dressed.

Full Membership List

HERRICK, GRETTE. Old Courthouse Studio and Gallery, 708 Salem Ave., Rolla, MO 65401. (573) 364-3212. Watercolor, specializing in edible wildflowers.

HUNTER, JILL. Hunter-Smith Handwovens, 604 Bonita Ave, Webster Groves, MO 63119. (314) 962-4408. Handwoven scarves and shawls and liturgical wear.

JACOBSMEYER, PEGGY. Fire-works, 944 Timber Glen Lane, Ballwin, MO 63021. (314) 230-6585. Original jewelry and sculpture in fused glass.

JACOBSON, TRUDY. Tea Berries, 7801 Wade School Road, Columbia, MO 65202-9665. (573) 442-5044. Antique-style bears in wood-resin designs, ornaments and figurines.

JEWSBURY, JEWELL ANN. Ozark Driftwood Santas, 1414 Euclid, Joplin, MO 64801. (417) 623-5695. Driftwood Santas with papier-mache beards on cups and sweatshirts.

JOHNSON, SHIRLEY. Spoonies, Inc., 2203 Thomas Rd., Norwood, MO 65717. (417) 746-4800. Historical wooden spoon dolls, paper dolls, video.

KUHN, CINDY. Cindy Kuhn Studio, 12794 W. Watson, Sunset Hills, MO 63127. (314) 843-4932. Whimsical furniture, painted treatments, custom-fired tile, sinks and dinnerware.

LeMAY, MARGOT. Calico, Court Square, 305 W. Third St., Rolla, MO 65401. (573) 364-2187. Ceramic Santas cast from Missouri clay slip.

LENTZ, RON. Ron Lentz Fine Woodworking, 2122 Victor Street, St. Louis, MO 63104. (314) 664-5940 or (314) 664-3531. Custom furniture, residential millwork, jewelry, and collectible boxes of hand-selected hardwoods.

LEONHARD, HEINRICH & IDA. Tannenbaum Ceramics, 218 E. Parkway, Columbia, MO 65203. (573) 449-1043. Ceramic Christmas and decorative ornaments, jewelry, bells and flutes.

MALLINSON, MELISSA. The Feather Merchant, Diamond M Farm, Rt. 1, Box 242, Princeton, MO 64673-9801. (816) 748-3558. Pheasant feather brooches and hair barrettes.

Full Membership List

MANVILLE, GEORGE & JAN. Rt. 5, Box 242A, Mexico, MO 65265. (573) 581-6755. Replicas of 17th-century watch boxes.

MARSHALL, NORMA. Feather Hill Arts, 8922 S. Hardsaw Rd., Oak Grove, MO 64075-7235. (816) 697-3466. Copper enamel jewelry.

MARTIN, BUENA. Buena Creations, P.O. Box 25904, St. Louis, MO 63136. (314) 385-2662. Brass and bead jewelry with ethnic flair.

McDONALD, JIM. JSK Creations in Wood, 4901 Highway D, Farmington, MO 63640. (573) 756-3239. Heirloom jewelry chests in Missouri woods.

MILLIGAN, DAVE & DEBBIE. The County Seat, 201 E. 4th St., Salem, MO 65560. (573) 729-8325. Custom furniture, staircases, woodworking.

MOORE, TONI. Artwork Originals, RR 2, Box 112, Downing, MO 63536-9535. (816) 379-2787 or (816) 379-2690.

MOYERS, MARY JANE. Touch from the Heart Pottery, Rt. 1, Box 76, Glen Allen, MO 63751. (573) 495-2553. Pottery.

NACHTRIEB, SHIRLEY ELEY. Shirley's Fine Art Studio, 908 Ruth Drive, St. Charles, MO 63301. (314) 947-1936. Watercolor portrait artist.

NEEF, FRANK. Pottery by Frank Neef, 1719 Hawthorne Rd., Highlandville, MO 65669. (417) 443-3861. Pottery.

OGLESBAY, COLLEEN & FLOYD. A Serendipity, 380 N. Roby Farm Road, Rocheport, MO 65279. (573) 449-8336 or (573) 874-0901. Hand-painted furniture and accent pieces. Woodworking, fretwork, furniture and gift items.

PAYNE, CAROLYN. Payne Creations in Tile, 4829 N. Antioch, Kansas City, MO 64119. (816) 452-8660. Architectural, murals for interior and exterior buildings, signage, gift and custom hand-painted tile.

PLATZ, HARRIET. Candles by Hawkins, 101 E. Walnut, P.O. Box 346, Shelbina, MO 63468. (573) 588-4008. Specializing in corn candles.

Full Membership List

POTTS, NENA. "NENA," 4205 E. Farm Rd. 172, Rogersville, MO 65742. (417) 886-7757. Fax (417) 886-9423. "Out of the Blue" line features birds, birdfeeders and birdhouse jewelry in silver, copper and brass. Simple, elegant contemporary designs in silver and niobium. Also does Missouri wildflower jewelry in painted leather.

RASA, BARBARA. The Apple Tree, Rt. 1, Box 122A, Higginsville, MO 64037. (816) 584-7379. Batik pictures, hand-dyed fabrics, hand-cast paper ornaments.

RATERMANN, MARTIN. Woodworker, 300 McRoberts Street, Boonville, MO 65233. (816) 882-2695. Fine custom woodwork and furniture.

RICHARDSON, ALLEN. Whole Bird Studio, 4350 E. Hillcrest Dr., Columbia, MO 65202. (573) 474-8104. Fibers, handmade turkey and pheasant feathers, paper, cards and journals.

SAUPE, DAVID & GARLYN. Grandview Woolens, 34560 Mabry Rd., Bucklin, MO 64631. (816) 695-3290. Wearable woolens — scarves, shawls, throws, hats and booties.

SCHRECKENGAST, BONNIE. B & L Baskets, 888 Schreckengast Rd., Wright City, MO 63390. (314) 745-3226. Hand-woven baskets, specializing in Cherokee Indian style weaving.

SELL, LISA. Weaving & Spinning, Rt. 1, Box 63, Elkland, MO 65644. (417) 933-5559. Functional wearable art. Specializes in pattern weaving and some historic patterns.

SMITH, KAREN ANNE. When Roses Bloom, 4501 South Sterling Ave., Kansas City, MO 64133, and P.O. Box 22614, Kansas City, MO 64113. (816) 358-1410. Pager (816) 247-9504.

SMITH, TARNEY. Tarney's Bailiwick, 915 West 7th St., Washington, MO 63090. (573) 239-1918. Reproduction Victorian Majolica ceramics, also "New Majolica."

SNYDER, HARRY. Village Pewter, 210 N. Central St., Rocheport, MO 65279-0150. (573) 698-2102. Traditional & contemporary lead-free pewter.

Full Membership List

SPANGLER, LEANDRA. Bear Creek Paperworks, 405 W. Texas, Columbia, MO 65202. (573) 442-3360. Journals, cards and one-of-a-kind sculptural vessels.

SPARKS, ANDREA & GERRY. Mastercraft Puppet, P.O. Box 39, Branson, MO 65615. (417) 561-8100. Top quality original puppets for home, school, church, special programs.

STEUCK, DAWN. Prairie Country, Rt. 3, Box 117, Rich Hill, MO 64779. (417) 395-4267. Authentic period, highly detailed corn husk dolls.

TAYLOR, ELAINE. Folk Art, 660 Riverview Rd., Labadie, MO 63055. (314) 742-4325. Wood carvings, sculpting and illustrations.

TAYLOR, JULIA, & DON SUMPTER. Woodworks FolkArt, HC88, Box 8536, Steelville, MO 65565. (573) 743-6627. Folk Art Ornaments, decorative spindles, candlesticks and other small works, limited edition fiber work.

THOMPSON, IDELL. Thompson's Funky Junque, Rt. 1, Box 197, Newtown, MO 64667. (816) 794-5651. Fine tatted lace.

WELTZIN, KATHLEEN & MICHAEL. Willow Works, 830 Marshall Avenue, Webster Groves, MO 63119. (314) 963-9417. Bent willow, white birch and twisted sassafras furniture and gifts for home, garden and lodge.

WESTON, JENNA. Gathering Root Basketry, Rt. 5, Box 934, Ava, MO 65608. (417) 683-3610. Unique baskets and sculptural vessels.

WYATT, DAVID. The Carpenter's Shop, 420 NW 51, Clinton, MO 64735. (816) 885-7700. Fine and handcrafted custom wood furniture.

YOUNG, ANNIE. Hidden Peace Farm, Rt. 1, Box 220, Meta, MO 65058. (573) 793-6613. Traditional and contemporary baskets using native Missouri materials.

YOUNG, ROSANNA L. Rag to 'Riginals, RR 7, Box 199, Poplar Bluff, MO 63901. (573) 778-9407. Re-creating dolls and clothing made from recycled clothing.

Associate Members

BARNES, CAROL, The Missouri Peddlers, Fairway Ct., Florissant, MO 63033. (314) 837-6923.

BAER-HUNSBURGER, CHRIS, 12519 East 41st Terrace, Independence, MO 64055-4463. (816) 373-1202.

COOK, NANCY, Paper Designs, 1 Bedford Ct., Bloomington, IL 61704.

CUNNINGHAM, BARBARA, Business & Industry Spec., University Extension, 1901 NE 48th St., Kansas City, MO 64118. (816) 792-7760, 792-7692.

DRAGSCHUTZ, VIRGINIA, 1 Oak Knoll, St. Charles, MO 63304. (314) 447-4935.

EXCLUSIVELY MISSOURI, Donna Leker, 200 S. W. Market, Lee's Summit, MO 64063. (816) 525-5747.

GRANT, SHIRLEY, Heart and Soul, 32772 Coates St. Rd., Macon, MO 63552. (816) 385-2542.

HEFNER, DIANNE, FanciFaux, Decorative Painting Studio, 5267 Cedarstone Court, Apt. B, St. Louis, MO 63129-2154. (314) 892-9680.

MISSOURI CREATIONS, 7 E. Dakota, Butler, MO 64844.

SAGER, TED & DEE, Wood Concepts, 314 N. Main, Granby, MO 64844. (417) 472-6852.

THWEATT, ANN, 402 N. Missouri, Nixa, MO 65714. (417) 725-3942.

WEST, PENNY, 2116A Louis Circle, Jefferson City, MO 65101. (314) 635-1467.

WOLKEN, CAMILLE & RICHARD, 703 Westmount Ave, Columbia, MO 65203-3472. (573) 449-4357.

Donors & Sponsoring Members

ASSOCIATED ELECTRIC COOPERATIVE, INC.
John Gulick, Community Development Specialist
2106 Jefferson,
P.O. Box 269
Jefferson City, MO 65102
(573) 634-2454

BLUESTEM MISSOURI CRAFTS
13 South Ninth,
Columbia, MO 65201
(573) 442-0211

Bluestem represents an extensive collection of fine crafts from Missouri and its neighboring states.

COLUMBIA PHOTO AND VIDEO
310 North Tenth,
Columbia, MO 65201
(573) 443-0503

Complete supply source for photographic equipment and services.

DORIS LITTRELL
Director of Extension Teaching
University of Missouri-Columbia
(573) 882-3598

1996 MABDA Board of Directors

President Nena Potts
Vice President Mary Benjamin
Treasurer Harry Snyder
Membership Secretary Barbara Rasa
New Membership Floyd and Colleen Oglesbay
New Membership Co-Chair Vickie Canham
Show Chairman Julia Taylor
Newsletter Editor/Acting Secretary Lee Ferber
Conference Chair Anne Crume
Conference Co-Chair Serena Boschert
Public Relations Kathleen Weltzin
Ex-Officio Edie Pigg
Ex-Officio Peggy Feagins

Advisory Board Members

Carole Barnes, Retail Advisor, St. Louis
Dr. Joe Stealey, Associate Professor of Art, UMC, Columbia
Barbara Cunningham, Business and Industry Specialist,
      University Extension, Kansas City
Sharon Gulick, Dept. of Economic Development,
      Manager of Business Information Programs, Jefferson City

Past Presidents of MABDA

Peggy Feagins
Thom Rakes
Serena Boschert
Lee Ferber

Annual Conference

ART SMART WEEKEND

Join us for our annual two-day seminar. Learn effective and indispensable marketing techniques to build a successful art business. The annual statewide conference is held each spring at the Rickman Conference Center in Jefferson City, Missouri.

What Is Art Smart Weekend?

It's a customized seminar designed specifically for and by artists who are serious about having a good time marketing their work. You don't want to miss this energy-filled conference! Learn creative strategies to reach diverse markets, develop skills for professional presentations, address technical business issues and network with craftspeople from all over Missouri.

"In addition to informative and motivational speakers, Best of Missouri Hands conferences provide an opportunity for one-on-one networking with a variety of business experts as well as other artists who are working through the same types of problems I face," said Nena Potts, president of MABDA and a member jeweler. "This exchange of ideas has played a big role in expanding my business and making me more professional."

For information about this year's conference
and/or an application, please contact:

Conference Chair
Best of Missouri Hands
P.O. Box 322
2101 West Broadway
Columbia, MO 65203

Membership Information

Q. What is the Missouri Artisans Business Development Association (MABDA)?

A. MABDA is a non-profit organization dedicated to providing creative and technical support for Missouri's art and craft community. It is governed by a board of directors who are members of the organization.

Q. What does the organization offer?

A. Membership brings artists valuable opportunities for marketing, educational and artistic growth, and professional development:
• The annual conference featuring national speakers, educational workshops and professional and social opportunities.
• A resource for sales opportunities, supplies, and up-to-date information on regional, national and international marketing opportunities.
• Access to business and creative workshops through the Missouri Artisan Educational Foundation (MAEF).
• A communication network for craftspeople, collectors, educators, retailers, students and suppliers throughout the state.

Q. How is MABDA supported?

A. This association is supported by artist membership fees, sponsoring individuals, organization fees and corporate and foundation grants.

Q. What are membership benefits?

A. All members receive a newsletter, reduced rates for conferences and workshops, a certificate of membership and a listing in the *Best of Missouri Hands*.

There are several levels of membership:

- Juried Member (Missouri resident $36) by slide review. Provides *Best of Missouri Hands* product labels and hangtags to use on your work. Eligibility for feature articles and photo page in *Best of Missouri Hands*, and access to state, regional, national and international marketing activities.
  - Student Member (full-time student $12)
  - Associate Member (non-juried $24)
  - Sponsoring Member ($100 or more)

For further information about the organization and membership, please contact:

New Membership Chair
Best of Missouri Hands
P.O. Box 322
2101 West Broadway
Columbia, MO 65203

Missouri Shops & Galleries

Columbia:

Bluestem Missouri Crafts
13 S. Ninth Street
Columbia, MO 65201
(573) 442-0211

Columbia Art League Gallery
1013 E. Walnut
Columbia, MO 65201
(573) 443-2131

Dauphine Art Gallery
918 E. Broadway Upstairs
Columbia, MO 65201
(573) 442-4457

I'd Rather Be Stamping
2529 Bernadette Drive
Columbia, MO 65203-4674
(573) 446-5930

Legacy Art & Book Works
1010 E. Broadway
Columbia, MO 65201
(573) 442-0855

Missouri Art Gallery
9 N. Tenth Street
Columbia, MO 65201
(573) 443-5010

Mythmaker Gallery
216 S. Fifth Street
Columbia, MO 65201
(573) 449-7870

Poppy
914 E. Broadway
Columbia, MO 65201
(573) 442-3223

Tucker's Fine Jewelry
& Gift Gallery
823 E. Broadway
Columbia, MO 65201
(573) 817-1310

Jefferson City:

Clan Vital Studio
122 E. High Street
Jefferson City, MO 65101
(573) 659-3610

Cottonstone Gallery
108 E. High St.
Jefferson City, MO 65101

Kansas City:

Cheri's Bear Essentials
3953 Broadway
KC, MO 64111
(816) 561-2018

Exclusively Missouri
200 S. W. Market
Lee's Summit, MO 64063
(816) 525-5747

The Muse Gallery
4142 Pennsylvania Ave.
KC, MO 64111
(816) 561-0810

Powell Gardens
1609 N.W. U.S. Highway 50
Kingsville, MO 64061
(816) 697-2600

Rustic Yearnings
Colonnade Shopping Center
17200 40 Highway
Independence, MO 64055
(816) 373-2423

Sebree Galleries
301 East 55th
KC, MO 64113
(816) 333-3387

The World's Window
4120 Pennsylvania Ave.
KC, MO 64111
(816) 454-4545

The Yako Gallery, Westport
4111 Pennsylvania Ave.
KC, MO 64111
(816) 756-2667

Rocheport:

A Serendipity
Missouri River City
380 N. Roby Farm Road
Rocheport, MO 65279
(573) 449-8336 and 874-0901

High Gate Gallery
501 Third Street
Rocheport, MO 65279
(573) 698-3207

Rocheport Gallery
204 2nd Street
Rocheport, MO 65279
(573) 698-2063

St. Louis:

Barucci Gallery
8101 Maryland
Clayton, MO 63105
(314) 272-2020

Craft Alliance
6640 Delmar Blvd.
St. Louis, MO 63101
(314) 725-1151

Art St. Louis
917 Locust
St. Louis, MO 63101
(314) 241-4810

The Gift Shoppe Limited
8817 Ladue
St. Louis, MO 63124
(314) 849-2213

The Greeting Gallery
8813 Ladue Road
Clayton, MO 63124
(314) 721-6263

Gypsies
325 S. Main
St. Charles, MO 63301
(314) 925-0033

Linda's Collectibles
409 S. Main
St. Charles, MO 63301
(314) 947-4076

Krueger Pottery
8153 Big Bend Boulevard
Webster Groves, MO 63119
(314) 963-6130

Meli-Melo
6635 Delmar Blvd.
St. Louis, MO 63130
(314) 725-4285

Missouri Botanical Garden
Gift Shop
4344 Shaw
St. Louis, MO 63110
(314) 577-5137

Old House in Hog Hollow
14319 Olive St. Rd.
Chesterfield, MO 63017
(314) 469-1019

Reflections of Missouri
903 South Main Street
St. Charles, MO 63301
(314) 946-1835

St. Charles Artists' Guild
524 S. Main
St. Charles, MO 63301
(314) 723-8009

The State Fare
Union Station
1820 Market Street
St. Louis, MO 63103
(314) 241-8664

Springfield:

Renaissance Books & Gifts
1337 F. Montclair
Springfield, MO 65804
(417) 883-5161

Showcase Galleries
1350 E. Battlefield
Springfield, MO 65804
(417) 887-2364

Springfield Art Museum Gift Shop
1111 E. Brookside Dr.
Springfield, MO 65807
(417) 837-5700

Spring House
4150 S. Lone Pine Ave.
Galloway Village 65804
Springfield, MO
(417) 887-8149

Traders Market
1845 E. Sunshine
Springfield, MO 65804
(417) 889-1145

Waverly House Gifts & Gallery
2031 S. Waverly
Springfield, MO 65804
(417) 882-3445

Other Missouri Galleries:

Artwork Originals Studio
Highway 136
Downing, MO 63536
(816) 379-2787

Big Cedar Lodge
612 Devil Pools Rd.
Ridgedale, MO 65739
(417) 335-2777

Bonadea Fine Artistries
239 S.E. Main
Lee's Summit, MO 64063
(816) 246-7275

The Classic Touch
529 Court Street
Fulton, MO 65251
(573) 642-9420

Cornerstone Fine Metals
& Jewelry Shop
Silver Dollar City
Branson, MO 65615
(417) 338-8216

Elm Street Company
301 Elm St.
Washington, MO 63090
(314) 239-1722

Firehouse Gallery
131 S. Central
Eureka, MO 63025
(314) 938-3303

Gallery On the Square
S.E. Corner of the Square
Lancaster, MO 63548
(816) 457-3161

Homestead Shoppe
111 N. Water Street
Liberty, MO 64068
(816) 781-7284

House of Mary B
Arrowrock, MO 65320
(816) 837-3305

Lynn's House of Art
601 Vine St.
Macon, MO 63552
(816) 385-6005

Main Street Antiques
111 E. Main Street
Steelville, MO 65565
(573) 775-3500

Moniteau Trader
Jamestown, MO 65046
(417) 849-2436

Touch-A-Heart Shop
Richmond, MO 64085
(816) 776-3131

The Trading Company of Defiance
2991 S. Highway 94
Defiance, MO 63341
(314) 987-2765

Wood'n Ya Want It
Tan Tara Resort
PO Box 188-TT
Osage Beach, MO 65065
(573) 348-3500

The Works Limited
80 S. Hwy Drive
Peerless Park, MO 63088
(314) 225-6446

Index

Acrylics, 38-39, 42-43, 48-49, 50-51, 68-69, 72-73, 96-97

Basketry, 30-31, 84-85, 100-101, 102-103

Batik, 78-79

Beads, 22-23, 26-27, 36-37, 40-41, 58-59

Boxes, 54-55, 60-61

Buttons, 4-5, 36-37, 58-59

Candles, 74-75

Candlesticks, 96-97

Caning, 30-31

Ceramic, 12-13, 34-35, 52-53, 56-57; tile, 18-19

Christmas ornaments, 18-19, 12-13, 34-35, 56-57, 96-97

Clay, 26-27, 32-33, 34-35, 50-51, 52-53; jewelry, 8-9, 46-47. *See also* Earthenware, Porcelain, Stoneware pottery, Terra cotta

Copper, 20-21

Dinnerware, 50-51, 88-89

Dolls, 48-49, 68-69, 86-87, 92-93

Earthenware, 12-13, 42-43

Fabrics, 6-7, 78-79

Feathers, 58-59

Fiber, dyes, 14-15, 78-79; wearable, 14-15, 36-37, 82-83, 96-97

Figurines, 46-47, 52-53

Flutes, 26-27

Found Objects, 22-23, 50-51

Frames, 6-7

Furniture, 6-7, 72-73; wood, 16-17, 50-51, 54-55, 64-65, 80-81, 98-99

Gemstones, 76-77; semi-precious, 22-23

Glass, 4-5, 10-11, 26-27, 40-41

Gold, 26-27, 76-77

Gourds, 38-39

Ink, 44, 94-95

Jewelry: clay, 8-9, 18-19, 34-35; other, 4-5, 20-21, 26-27, 40-41, 59-60, 76-77; wood, 46-47, 54-55

Latex, 50-51

Leather, 76-77

132 — *Best of Missouri Hands*

Looms, 14-15

Metals, 16-17, 76-77

Oils, 48-49, 66-67, 72-73

Ornaments, 26-27, 28-29, 46-47, 96-97. *See also* Christmas ornaments

Paper, 78-79, 90-91; making, 24-25, 100-101. *See also* Scherenschnitte

Papier-mache, 94-95

Pastels, 68-69

Pewter, 4-5, 88-89

Porcelain, 4-5, 8-9, 18-19, 70-71; dolls, 86-87

Portraits, 12-13, 66-67, 68-69

Reed, 30-31, 84-85, 101-2

Scherenschnitte, 6-7

Silver, 20-21, 26-27, 40-41, 76-77

Spinning, 14-15

Stone, 16-17

Stoneware pottery, 26-27, 32-33, 34-35

Tapestries, 14-15

Teddy bears, 46-47

Terra cotta, 86-87

Vases, 10-11

Wall hangings, 100-101

Watch boxes, 60-61

Watercolors, 44-45, 68-69, 72-73

Wax, 74-75

Weaving, 14-15

Wildflowers, 10-11, 36-37, 76-77; paintings of, 44-45

Wildlife, 66-67, 76-77

Wind chimes, 35

Wire mesh, 28-29

Wood, 30, 98-99, 100-101; carving, 2-3, 94-95, 96-97; furniture, 16-17, 50-51, 54-55, 64-65, 72-73, 80-81; resin, 46-47; watchcases, 60-61

Dufur — 133

Show Me Missouri books are available at many local bookstores. They can also be ordered directly from the publisher, using this form, or ordered by phone, fax or over the Internet.

Pebble Publishing also distributes 100 other books of regional interest, rails-to-trails, Missouri history, heritage, nature, recreation and more. These are available through our online bookstore and a seasonal mail-order catalog. Visit our online bookstore, called *Trailside Books* at http://www.trailsidebooks.com, or leave a message at pebble@global-image.com. If you would like to receive our catalog, please fill out and mail the form on the next page.

The Show Me Missouri Series

The Complete Katy Trail Guidebook
By Brett Dufur
ISBN: 0-9646625-0-7

The most complete guide to services, towns, people, places and history along Missouri's 200-mile Katy Trail. This updated second edition book covers the cross-state hiking and biking trail from Sedalia to St. Charles. Includes trailhead maps, 80 photos, Flood of '93, how to make blueberry wine, uses for Missouri mud and more. 144 pages.

What's That? A Nature Guide to the Missouri River Valley
Compiled by Brett Dufur
ISBN: 0-9646625-1-5

Companion guide to the *Katy Trail Guidebook.* This easy-to-use, richly illustrated four-season guide identifies trees, flowers, birds, animals, insects, rocks, fossils, clouds, reptiles, footprints and more. Also features the Missouri River Valley's most outstanding sites and nature daytrips. 176 pages.

Wit & Wisdom of Missouri's Country Editors
By William Taft
ISBN: 0-9646625-3-1

A compilation of over 600 pithy sayings from pioneer Missouri newspapers, when editors were forceful in their opinions, unaffected by today's politically correct philosophy. Many of these quotes and quips date to the 19th century yet remain timely for today's readers. Richly illustrated and fully indexed to help you find that perfect quote. 168 pages.

A to Z Missouri: The Dictionary of Missouri Place Names
By Margot Ford McMillen
ISBN: 0-9646625-4-X

Tightwad, Paris, Peculiar, Whoop-Up and more! A dictionary-style book of Missouri place name origins. Includes history for each town and community, pronunciations, population, county, post office dates and more. 220 pages.

99 Fun Things to Do in Columbia & Boone County
By Pamela Watson
ISBN: 0-9646625-2-3

Guide to 99 hidden highlights, unique dining, galleries, museums, towns, people and history in Columbia, Rocheport, Centralia and Boone County. Most trips are free or under $10. Includes maps, photos, accessibility of sites. Fully indexed. 168 pages.

Best of Missouri Hands
By Brett Dufur
ISBN: 0-9646625-5-8

Profiles of Missouri's fine artists and craftsmen. From porcelain to wood and pewter to gold, *Best of Missouri Hands* shows the best our state has to offer. With over 125 artists listed, this book highlights many traditional art forms and techniques, and the artists behind the expressions. 144 pages.

Quantity

____ KT Guidebook	x $14.95 =	_____
____ Nature Guide	x $14.95 =	_____
____ 99 Fun Things	x $12.95 =	_____
____ Wit & Wisdom	x $14.95 =	_____
____ A to Z Missouri	x $14.95 =	_____
____ Best of Missouri Hands	x $12.95 =	_____
Mo. residents add 6.975% sales tax	=	_____
Shipping ($1.24 each book) x	=	_____
	Total =	_____

Name:_____
Address:_____ Apt._____
City, State, Zip_____
Phone: (____) _____
   Credit Card # _____
   Expiration Date ____/____/____   Please send catalog _____

Send (or photocopy and send) this page to:

Pebble Publishing

P.O. Box 431 ❖ Columbia, MO 65205-0431
(800) 576-7322 ❖ Fax: (573) 698-3108
Visit our *Trailside Books* online
at http://www.trailsidebooks.com

Special thanks to the MABDA Book Committee:
Mary Benjamin, Vickie Canham, Meg Gibson, Carol Leigh Brack-Kaiser, Colleen and Floyd Oglesbay, Edie Pigg and Harry Snyder.

Project support by Pebble Publishing staff:
R. C. Adams, Brett Dufur, Daisy Dufur, Pippa Letsky, Mary Mueller, Jan Parenteau, Heather Starek, Kristie Trock and Jillian Watson.

Cover photograph of vessel by Frank Neef. Photograph by Brett Dufur. Additional photo credits: Toni Moore pages 66-67; Karen Smith pages 86-87; Rick Truax page 88 and vertical on back cover; Doug Ziegler p. 26.

Book masthead design by Jim Sadler.

ISBN 0-9646625-5-8 12.95
Copyright © 1996 by MABDA. All other rights © 1996 Pebble Publishing

All rights reserved. No part of this book may be reproduced, stored in a retrieval system, or transmitted in any form or by any means, electronic, mechanical, photocopying, recording or otherwise, without express written consent from the publisher.

Remit all correspondence to:
Best of Missouri Hands
P.O. Box 322
2101 West Broadway
Columbia, MO 65203

Quantity and wholesale book orders (minimum 12) should be directed to:
Best of Missouri Hands
c/o Pebble Publishing
P.O. Box 431
Columbia, MO 65205-0431

Printed by Ovid Bell Press, Inc., of Fulton, Missouri, USA